INVESTIGATING

# MURDOCH
## MYSTERIES

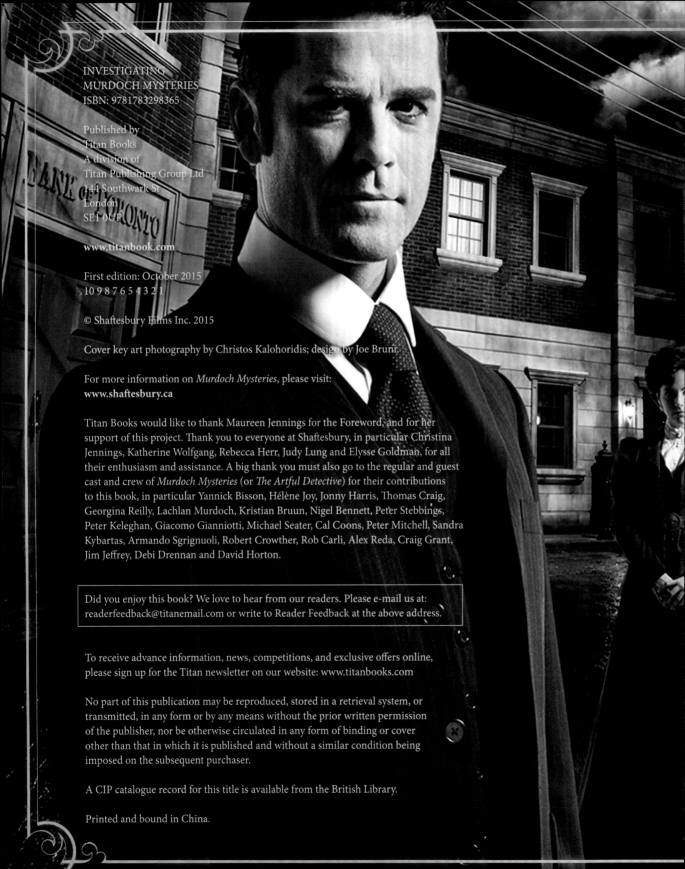

INVESTIGATING
MURDOCH MYSTERIES
ISBN: 9781783298365

Published by
Titan Books
A division of
Titan Publishing Group Ltd
144 Southwark St
London
SE1 0UP

www.titanbook.com

First edition: October 2015
10 9 8 7 6 5 4 3 2 1

Cover key art photography by Christos Kalohoridis; design by Joe Bruni.

For more information on *Murdoch Mysteries*, please visit:
**www.shaftesbury.ca**

Titan Books would like to thank Maureen Jennings for the Foreword, and for her support of this project. Thank you to everyone at Shaftesbury, in particular Christina Jennings, Katherine Wolfgang, Rebecca Herr, Judy Lung and Elysse Goldman, for all their enthusiasm and assistance. A big thank you must also go to the regular and guest cast and crew of *Murdoch Mysteries* (or *The Artful Detective*) for their contributions to this book, in particular Yannick Bisson, Hélène Joy, Jonny Harris, Thomas Craig, Georgina Reilly, Lachlan Murdoch, Kristian Bruun, Nigel Bennett, Peter Stebbings, Peter Keleghan, Giacomo Gianniotti, Michael Seater, Cal Coons, Peter Mitchell, Sandra Kybartas, Armando Sgrignuoli, Robert Crowther, Rob Carli, Alex Reda, Craig Grant, Jim Jeffrey, Debi Drennan and David Horton.

Did you enjoy this book? We love to hear from our readers. Please e-mail us at: readerfeedback@titanemail.com or write to Reader Feedback at the above address.

To receive advance information, news, competitions, and exclusive offers online, please sign up for the Titan newsletter on our website: www.titanbooks.com

A CIP catalogue record for this title is available from the British Library.

Printed and bound in China.

# INVESTIGATING
# MURDOCH
# MYSTERIES

## THE OFFICIAL COMPANION TO THE SERIES

MICHELLE RICCI
WITH MIR BAHMANYAR

TITANBOOKS

# Contents

# Acknowledgments

I have been lucky enough to work as a writer on *Murdoch Mysteries* since season 5. In that time I have come to appreciate the incredible and almost superhuman effort by cast and crew to pull off our ambitious scripts, in a short amount of time and on a budget. It can only happen when everyone involved cares as much as the Murdoch crew does, a rare phenomenon in this industry. But to everyone involved with the show, it is so much more than a pay cheque. It is a family, and work that each and every person is proud to be a part of.

The one refrain we heard over and over when interviewing cast and crew for this book is how much they all love to work on Murdoch. I, of course, agree. Actors are thrilled to be cast on the show, and often talk about what a great place it is to visit. Crew request to be put on the show, because of the great atmosphere and the fun challenges. It's not every show that goes from a zombie attack to an underground screwing machine to a moving picture show and beyond.

There are a great many people who work very hard to make a TV show, and Murdoch Mysteries has perhaps the hardest working crew of all. Writing this book took almost as many people, and we have to thank everyone who took the time to talk to us, answer our

emails and offer their support for this endeavour, even during their holidays and while the show is on hiatus:

Yannick Bisson, Hélène Joy, Jonny Harris, Thomas Craig, Georgina Reilly, Lachlan Murdoch, Arwen Humphreys, Kristian Bruun, Nigel Bennett, Peter Stebbings, Peter Keleghan, Giacomo Gianniotti, Michael Seater, Cal Coons, Sandy Kybartas, Armando Sgrignuoli, Craig Grant, Rob Carli, Kristjan Bergey, Alex Reda, Robert Crowther, Jim Jeffrey, Debi Drennan, Peter Mitchell, Paul Aitken, Carol Hay, Simon McNabb, Jordan Christianson, Yuri Yakubiw, Diane Kerbel, David Horton, Don McCutcheon, Stephen Montgomery, Tina Vacalopoulos and everyone at Shaftesbury.

A special thank you to Katherine Wolfgang for her willingness to answer emails at midnight, and her endless support as we tried to pull this book together in a very short amount of time.

Thank you to cast and crew for caring, and for making a show that has brought families together and shown Canada to the world.

And the biggest thank you of all goes to the fans in Canada and across the globe. We at *Murdoch Mysteries* love what we do, and we are thrilled there are so many people out there who love it too.

*Michelle Ricci and Mir Bahmanyar*

# Foreword

It is dark and cold and I'm watching a scene being filmed for the episode 'Shipwreck'. This is the first solo script I have written for the show and it's an adaptation from my novella about Detective William Murdoch as a boy.

We are using special towers which fling out water to simulate heavy rain. There are two enormous industrial fans blowing said water. There is palpable urgency all around. The shoot is in overtime and the producer has said there can be only one take. The fictional story is also full of urgency as Father Keegan, together with young Murdoch and some villagers, tries to save the crew of a foundering ship. The priest and the boy run down the cliff holding their lanterns aloft, the lights swaying and bobbing. The beach is in reality a gravel pit, but the darkness is real, the cold is real and the actors are getting soaked to the skin. Nobody makes a mistake. The take is successful.

Watching this come together, fiction and reality, is one of the absolute highlights of my life. My story dramatized in such a brilliant way. My characters brought to life. Who'd have thought it?

I attended Assumption University, [Ontario, Canada,] which was run by the Basilian Fathers. Some of my teachers had a huge impact on me. One in particular demanded that his students *think*. Don't just regurgitate – think, question, ponder, all those sort of words. I took that to heart and later, when Murdoch was coming into being, I gave him those characteristics. He can seem quite priest-like at times, including being celibate, this because I wanted to be true to the times he lives in. Sexual activity outside of marriage was frowned upon. There was the ubiquitous double standard; men could do what women couldn't, but it wasn't easy for a man of principle like Murdoch to find a partner outside of marriage. So he doesn't. (Or does he?)

The deeply entrenched lines of the British class structure are familiar, but also long standing is the divide between Catholic and Protestant. My mother was originally from an Irish Catholic background, my father was pallid Church of England. I liked creating a Catholic detective and putting him in a city so completely WASP [white Anglo-Saxon Protestant] as Victorian Toronto. He is perforce a perpetual outsider and that has its advantages.

Because of what I knew about childhood influences, I gave Murdoch a troubled early life. An alcoholic father, a mother who dies suddenly and mysteriously, a beloved sister who escapes to a convent. He suffers from loneliness. This is mitigated by his intense curiosity about the world and his constant seeking for solutions to the problems he encounters.

In my own uncertain childhood, a policeman on his beat was considered a friend, a protector. Not surprisingly, perhaps, Murdoch is that kind of policeman.

*Maureen Jennings*

# Introduction

One of the ways that Shaftesbury has built its reputation is by adapting novels. So when the publisher of Maureen Jennings (no relation to me) sent us books, now over twelve years ago, I was keen to read. I loved the idea of a detective set in Toronto at the turn of the twentieth century. That was a unique angle. And I loved the idea of this central character, Detective William Murdoch, as a Catholic in a Protestant city. A true "fish out of water" that as a central character is so interesting to watch.

At the time, our company was making television movies, so we decided to adapt three of Maureen's books to see what the market thought of this character and this world. The adaptations were quite faithful to the books, with one exception: it was important to me to have a central female character in the mix. I liked the idea of finding a character who, like Murdoch, is operating outside of her comfort zone – in this case, a female coroner in a man's world. This became the character of Julia Ogden.

The three movies were very successful in Canada, but also gained an international following, especially in the UK and France. Our broadcaster at the time asked us to consider building on the TV movie franchise by creating a continuing series. For North America at the time, this was really an "out of the box" request. People loved contemporary stand-alone cop series (*CSI* was at the start of its heyday), but to set a procedural series at the turn of the century was unheard of.

So, we started to develop the TV series. I wanted it to be somewhat of a departure from the movies. I wanted the books to celebrate the extraordinary times that were the Victorian era. Anything was possible. The age of steampunk. I wanted the series to resonate with today's younger audiences. I wanted the series to have humour, especially in the banter between our characters. I wanted today's audience to see the "nods" we were giving to the future. And there were so many. I wanted romance. We had two wonderful central characters in Murdoch and Ogden, both testing their limits and working alongside one another on cases. Of course they would be drawn together. That has become part of the fun of the series – the "on and off again" – the "will they, won't they" dynamic between them.

Producers are only as good as the team around them. It always starts with the words – Maureen's books and the wonderful writers that are on the show (some almost from the beginning). The words then flow to the actors who bring the characters to life, led by Yannick, Hélène, Thomas, Jonny, Georgina and all the others. The actors are guided by the directors. And all of it lives thanks to the efforts of the hundreds of craftspeople who

recreate Toronto at the turn of the twentieth century.

We have assembled an amazing family with this series. Thank you to Michelle Ricci and Mir Bahmanyar for working tirelessly to share their stories in this beautiful book. And thank you to Jo Boylett and the entire team at Titan Books for bringing this project to life.

If someone had told me twelve years ago, as I read Maureen's first book, that I would be making *Murdoch Mysteries* all these years later, and that this Toronto/Canadian world and characters would resonate with audiences around the world, I would have told them, "Dream on." But, hey, dreams sometimes do come true.

*Christina Jennings*
Chairman & CEO, Shaftesbury
Executive Producer, *Murdoch Mysteries*

# Creating the World of
# MURDOCH MYSTERIES

**Constable George Crabtree** *"**The Filmed Adventures of Detective William Murdoch** hardly trips off the tongue, and it would make for a very long marquee."*

**Detective William Murdoch** *"That's true."*

**James Pendrick** *"What do you suggest?"*

**Crabtree** *"**Just** The Murdoch Mysteries."*

**Pendrick** *"I like it."*

KEITH        BRODSKI
DAVID        COATSWORTH
ANDREW       CRAWFORD
GRAHAM       DUNN
DAVID        GROPMAN
JAMES        HALPENNY
DOUGLAS      INGLE
FERD         IONSON
TROY         JENKS
DEAN         MIRSKI
DON          RETZER
VICTOR       RIGLER
STEVEN       SHEWCHUK
JAMES        STERNBERG
PETER        WENZEL

*Inspector Thomas Brackenreid (Thomas Craig), Detective William Murdoch (Yannick Bisson), Dr Julia Odgen (Hélène Joy)*
*and Constable George Crabtree (Jonny Harris) in a season 1 promotional photo.*

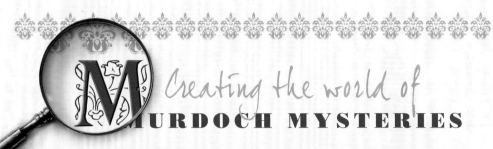

*Georgina Reilly (Dr Emily Grace) and Thomas take a break between scenes for 'Toronto's Girl Problem' (814) on location in St. Marys, ON.*

*Murdoch Mysteries* is beloved by fans around the world for its charm, ripping mysteries, steampunk-style inventions, scientific bent and aspirational characters. This world that has been created by a great many people over the years has become an integral part of daily life to many viewers, the characters like family and the sets a second home. This book is a glimpse into what makes *Murdoch Mysteries* the show it is, and why fans and cast and crew are so happy to be a part of it.

*Murdoch, Brackenreid and Crabtree test out the pneumograph, Murdoch's handmade lie detector (108).*

The Victorian (1837-22 January 1901) through Edwardian (23 January 1901-1910) eras were a time of great industrial and scientific advancement, proving the ideal setting for Detective William Murdoch, a man with a scientific mind and a true heart. His intellectual equal is city coroner-turned-psychiatrist Dr Julia Ogden, an upper-class, intelligent forward-thinker who does not buckle under social convention. They share a mutual respect, and a love of science and invention. They also share a great love for each other, despite the difficulties, and their love is one for the ages.

Though Murdoch places himself on the cutting edge of forensic advancements and has an ingenious way of solving crimes, his boss Inspector Thomas Brackenreid is a product of the old school; policing through brute force. He and Murdoch may not agree on how to solve a case, but they have a grudging respect for each other, one that grows into genuine friendship. Despite Brackenreid's reliance on his fists, at Station No. 4 there are more thinkers than not. Constable George Crabtree is Murdoch's right hand man. Uneducated but thoughtful and a thoroughly decent man, Crabtree proves a useful sidekick. He is a quick learner and eager to share with Murdoch his unusual theories, a source of frustration for Murdoch, but constant amusement for everyone else. He meets his match in Dr Emily Grace, a late arrival to the team, who takes over Ogden's position in the morgue. An idealist and feminist, Grace loves to solve the puzzle inherent in a dead body. She is fearless and sometimes careless, willing to try anything, without a thought to the consequences.

*Above: Crabtree and Grace are in awe of the film production.*

*Main: Grace and Murdoch soon ascertain that Prescott (Jefferson Brown) has been shot for real (703).*

The five main characters are supported by various friends and foes, and are visited by some of the most famous and influential historical figures of the time. Murdoch and his colleagues sometimes find themselves unwitting inventors of aspects of modern life, in a charming nod to the audience.

# THE VISION FOR THE SERIES

The police take Fannie Robinson (Mariah Inger) into custody (103).

Brackenreid puts the finishing touches on Murdoch's "Oscar Wilde" undercover disguise (105).

After the television movies of Maureen Jennings' books, the decision was made to turn *Murdoch Mysteries* into a continuing television series. Cal Coons, writer and showrunner, was brought into the series part way through the development of the TV show. He immediately coined a phrase that has endured as the mantra of the writers' room throughout its many seasons: "more Jules Verne, less Dickens."

Cal wanted to set the series in a world full of possibility, with an eye toward the future and the show was taken into a lighter, brighter place than its previous filmed incarnation. The plan was to focus on cultural and scientific advancements, and to make the central character, William Murdoch, the embodiment of that promise of a better world.

The show also demonstrated its flexibility in that first season. The tone could range from the very serious and dark to the fantastical, a range that has been exploited throughout its eight seasons. As long as the show stayed centred around the grounded and sensible character of Detective Murdoch, the murder could take him anywhere, into any world, no matter how tragic or absurd.

*Things go awry at the Alternating Current presentation (101).*

There was some concern in 2007, when the series was being developed, that period drama was not in fashion. There were no major television series that had a similar tone or setting, so no one quite knew if an audience could be found for this unique show. The mysteries would have to be compelling, the settings new and interesting, and the characters and cast appealing. The writing staff embraced the challenge. Victorian Toronto gave them the opportunity to tell stories with a fresh perspective. Research became key, to ground each story in an historically accurate setting. *Murdoch Mysteries* was now not only entertaining, but a window into a bygone time, and a slice of Canadian history that intrigued and resonated with audiences around the world.

Though Victorian Toronto was a very different place, the issues of the day were not so far from modern times. The writers realized they could use the era as a nice parallel to Toronto today, and stories that originated as Canadian but felt universal became the backbone of the series.

## VICTORIAN TORONTO

Toronto at the turn of the nineteenth century was the second largest city in Canada, with a population of 181,000 in 1891, growing slightly to 208,040 in 1901. Unlike today, Murdoch's Toronto was not a cultural mosaic. The inhabitants were largely of British descent, with only a very small percentage of western Europeans and African-Canadians. Immigrants outside of the English middle classes were typically poor labourers, destined for manual labour and life in The Ward, a shanty-town in the area of Toronto's current city hall. The city had a rigid class system, despite the lack of a true aristocracy. Toronto was very much modelled after Queen Victoria's ideal. Propriety and social convention ruled the population. But a spirit of independence bubbled underneath.

Racial and religious tensions were very much a part of Toronto life. The city was chiefly English Protestant and positions of power throughout the city were held by Protestant men. Catholics were considered second class citizens, and were tolerated only as such. Although the city did have a very small Jewish population, they had no place in society outside of their small businesses. No other major religion was widely practiced at the time. That would all come many years later.

But it wasn't all work all the time in Victorian Toronto. Vaudeville theatres, penny arcades, the amusement park at Hanlan's Point, the beaches in the summer and ice skating in the winter, were open to all. The upper class also enjoyed the opera, ballet, theatre, balls and galas, in the English tradition.

*Rowena Beaton (Stephanie Langton, bottom left), Beaton housekeeper (Maureen Jennings, top left), Ronald Beaton (Jordan Pettle, bottom centre), Claire (Marium Carvell, bottom right) and the rest of the staff are questioned about the murder at Beaton Manor (310).*

# TORONTO POLICE FORCE

**1859 SAW THE LANDMARK FORMATION** of the first Board of Commissioners of Police in Toronto, removing the force from the jurisdiction of the Toronto City Council. The board included the city's mayor and police magistrate, and introduced discipline and standards into the service when its new Chief of Police quickly moved to standardize training and hiring practices.

The subsequent years up to 1895 – when our television series begins – were marked by various firsts and improvements. They included the use of the telegraph to link stations within the city, and later the installation of the first call box, as well as the introduction of all-night patrols and of a mounted unit to patrol outlying areas (and control speeding horses), in 1894 of bicycles for patrols, and in 1895 the first Toronto police boat. A police benefit fund was set up in 1880.

During that same period, the focus of the police force also shifted. Initially set up primarily to suppress rebellion in the city, specifically of the working classes, it gradually moved to policing the city's morals. It had also been the main source of "social services" until just before Murdoch's time, when the creation of the Toronto Humane Society in 1887 and Children's Aid Society in 1891 took on overseeing animal and child welfare respectively. However, the police continued to operate the city's ambulance service, provide housing for the homeless, regulate (and license) street-level business, and censor all forms of public entertainment and literature in Toronto well into the twentieth century.

## Did You Know?

A "prop" is considered to be anything any of the actors will touch or handle during a scene. So money, newspapers, telephones, typewriters, wallets, food, firearms and so on are all provided by the props department, and on *Murdoch Mysteries* this is in addition to whatever crazy invention *Murdoch* has cooked up that week!

*Simon Brooks (Percy Hynes White) gets caught pickpocketing by Crabtree (818).*

Discrimination was not yet a bad word. Poor children roamed the streets, begging or pickpocketing. Newsboys worked for pennies. Just as the world was exploding with scientific advancements and innovations, so too were con men and women exploiting these innovations with quack inventions of their own, claiming all sorts of false benefits for a price. Honesty and righteousness were qualities reserved for those who could afford to have them.

But Toronto was by most standards, a safe, quiet city. There was very little crime beyond the petty. Public drunkeness, pickpocketing and, occasionally, licentious behaviour made up the majority of infractions. The nickname "Toronto the Good" implied a certain moral standard within the city. Toronto was also known as the Queen City and the city of churches. The people were hard working, loyal to the crown, pious and good. At least on the surface.

In Toronto, the people of the late Victorian era felt an optimism, and a momentum forward. The entire future was at their disposal. A young country, a city destined to become world class, and an era of invention and progress exploding all around it. The ideal time and place for Detective William Murdoch, a product of propriety and a believer in progress, to become our window into the era that began the thrust into the modern world as we know it.

*Josef Karnaki (Robin Kasyanov) readies a new sinister weapon based on Tesla's theories (313).*

*Above: Thomas Craig and Yannick Bisson shoot a scene on the backlot (603).*

*Right: Extras on the backlot for the same episode (603).*

# Recreating
## VICTORIAN TORONTO

## THE SETS

Toronto today is not an easy place to shoot a television series set over one hundred years ago. Busy streets, modern signage and altered architecture make it nearly impossible to find a location that can be made to look as it used to be. The production team knew they were going to need to build the parts of Murdoch's world that he would be inhabiting the most. The police station was to be where Murdoch would spend most of his time. It needed to fulfil the practical needs of shooting a television show, and it needed to look and feel like a Toronto police station of the 1890s.

When Sandy Kybartas was brought on as the production designer for the series, she already had one Murdoch television movie under her belt. Police Station No. 4 was already mostly formed in her head. The challenge was to bring her design to life and recreate the Victorian era – a time of sumptuous fabrics and detailed decor – on a budget.

Police Station No. 4 was modelled after real historical photos of police stations in Toronto from the 1890s. The references Sandy and her team used spanned several years, allowing them to take the best of the historically accurate architecture and layout in order to evoke the era. Knowing the police station would be a key set, where pivotal scenes for both character and plot would take place, Sandy tuned into her natural instinct for orthogonal design, with its use of right angles and straight lines. The Victorian era was reflected in this rigidity of form, and the standard rooms and right angles allowed for maximum use of space for the decor as well as the more practical needs.

*Yannick Bisson, Prime Minister Stephen Harper and Jonny Harris prepare to film Harper's cameo appearance as Desk Sergeant Armstrong (407).*

A set must do three things: build the world, support the actors and allow the crew to do their jobs. A director needs as many perspectives as possible to choose from to allow the camera to capture and enhance the words on the page. A cinematographer needs space for lighting, and enough distance from the actors to manipulate the lighting and shadows to support the director's vision of the scene. The crew need room to move, set up and store equipment, and sometimes places to hide when called upon to carry out a task off-camera while the actors are performing. The actors need the set to reinforce their characters, and help them to become another person from another time. After all of this is taken into consideration – and perhaps its most important function – a set also needs

# POLICE STATION № 4

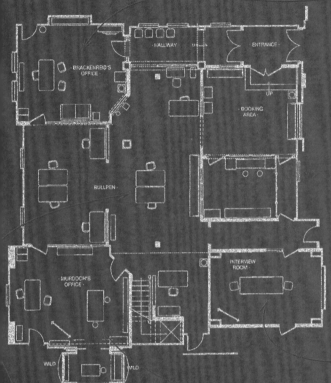

*Brackenreid in his office (413).*

*Pierre Barnett (Bruce Dow) is questioned by Murdoch in the interview room (307).*

*Arrested circus performers wait in the bullpen (307).*

*Inspector Edward Scanlon (Alastair Mackenzie) and Murdoch in Murdoch's office (202).*

to transport the audience out of their living rooms and into the world of the show, fully and seamlessly, each and every week.

Sandy made sure the police station fulfilled all of these criteria. Walls and different sections provided several different areas in which to shoot scenes: a booking area with a raised desk for a sergeant to admit criminals and citizens alike, a bullpen where the constables would work at desks and typewriters, benches for witnesses and complainants, offices for Inspector Brackenreid and Detective Murdoch, two hallways and an interview room, kept spartan to allow focus on the actors during those key interrogation scenes. Understanding that the distance the camera can see behind the action, or depth of field, is what gives a set a feeling of realism, Sandy used windows to line the walls of Brackenreid and Murdoch's offices and to separate the booking area from the bullpen. These windows allow a director to shoot from one corner of the police station and see almost all the way to the other end. The audience would still have a sense of a bustling police station no matter what Murdoch was doing, isolated in his office. The world around Murdoch could keep moving, and the audience could believe they were truly transported back in time.

*The set is almost a museum of the show at this point. I like to walk around and see all the different props and set dressing accumulated over the years.*

Lachlan Murdoch, *Constable Henry Higgins*

In the first season, *Murdoch Mysteries* took over a studio on Eastern Avenue in Toronto. The space in that studio was such that Sandy and her team needed every square inch to build the very important police station. But the scripts also called for a morgue; a morgue that would be second in importance only to the police station and would see plenty of action on its own. Sandy and her art director, Armando Sgrignuoli, set about finding a place in the already full studio for the morgue. They had six feet to spare on the side of the police station set, then the floor dipped significantly, resembling a pit, to provide access to the loading bay doors of the building. This imperfect space was their only option. Part of the morgue could be built flush with the police station, but the sunken floor meant either filling it in, at considerable expense, or building it into the design. Sandy and Armando chose the latter, and found it worked to their advantage. They used the descent from Ogden's office at the top of the stairs to the examination area below to evoke a subliminal suggestion of descending from life unto death. Much as Murdoch will use whatever he has at his disposal to build an invention or solve a case, so Sandy and Armando used what they had to build a beautiful and functional set, with an unique design that enhances the action and allows for more interesting filming than if the set had been all on one level.

# MORGUE

*Behind-the-scenes photo showing the view from the morgue's office window over the examination area.*

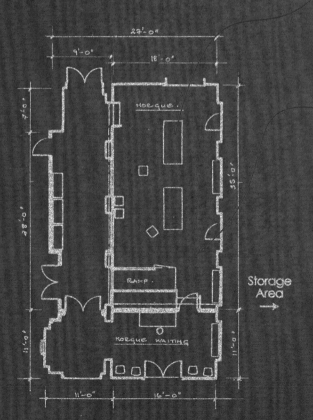

*The examination area (108).*

*Grace and Crabtree in the morgue (504).*

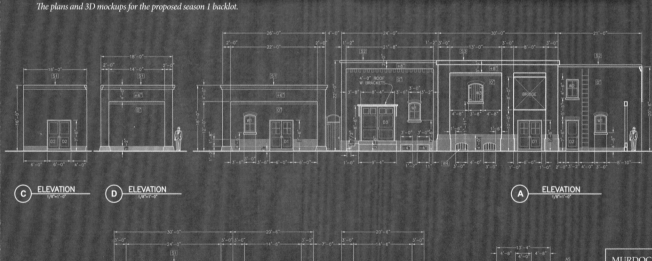

*The plans and 3D mockups for the proposed season 1 backlot.*

MURDOC•
MYSTERI•

Production Designer:
Sandra Kybartas
Drawing:
ELEVATIONS A,B

ALLEY WAY

629 EASTERN AVE.
OUTSIDE STUDIO K
Scale:
1/8"=1'-0"
Drawn By:
M Navarrete
Issued: APRIL 17/07
Sheets:

Dwg No.:
2.0

Detail and atmosphere are key parts of *Murdoch Mysteries'* success in evoking the Victorian and Edwardian eras. Visitors to the sets often remark on the level of detail, from the photos and wanted posters on the walls of the police station, to the unfinished report in Crabtree's typewriter, to the relevant letters on the desk in Ogden's asylum office, to the numerous jars of chemicals and poisons in the morgue. The camera may not always find all of these details, but somehow they are still seen, be it through the actors completely immersed in a bygone time, or the audience's subconscious awareness of them. Armando tells his team that when they are dressing a set they "have to be able to smell it." In effect, the visual sense created must simulate all the other senses, to make the audience think they can smell the coal burning in the stove, even if no one says so.

**The crew on Murdoch Mysteries *is one of the happiest crews in the industry.*** Cal Coons, *Executive Producer*

In the beginning, dressing the sets was a challenge. Sourcing antique items in Canada is not always easy. The Canadian Broadcasting Corporation once had an entire department devoted to the acquisition and maintenance of period items to use in their own productions. They had decades worth of accumulated period furniture, window dressings, fabrics, adornments, lighting and all the necessary set dressing Sandy and Armando could ever want. Fortuitously, at exactly the time *Murdoch Mysteries* was preparing to begin filming, the CBC was in the process of selling off their vast stores of antique Canadiana. The show was more than happy to take this valuable treasure trove off their hands, and continue to use it, much as CBC had done, to bring historic Canada back to life. The vastness of the collection has given *Murdoch* its richness, variation and depth of detail, and it is only fitting that it should have come from the CBC, Canada's public broadcaster and now *Murdoch Mysteries'* home network.

Shooting on location has always been a challenge for *Murdoch Mysteries*. There are few places that can be quickly restored to their original nineteenth century glory, and the exteriors of streets and buildings provide even more challenges, with all the modern additions. Although a dedicated backlot – an exterior set built on studio property or the "back lot" of the building – didn't make its way onto the show until season 5, there were plans to build a small section of street and alley for easy exterior shooting in season 1. Sandy and Armando went so far as to complete 3D mockups of what it could have been. Ultimately, the plans to build it were abandoned, and the series went on location to shoot their exterior scenes to the smaller towns outside the Toronto area, like Cambridge and Hamilton, where more Victorian architecture had been preserved.

In Season 5 *Murdoch Mysteries* moved their production to Sullivan Studios, which had a dedicated period backlot already built. Unfortunately, the backlot was built to serve as a small country town in the 1920s. Not exactly the brick and stone work of Toronto at the turn of the twentieth century. While not all of it was preserved, the production team refaced a small section of the existing backlot, including an area that became the never-before-seen back entrance to Police Station No. 4, and front entrance loading doors to the City Morgue. Several shops line the streets, with glass displays that can be changed as necessary, from a butcher to a barber to a grocer and more. Fruit carts, portable advertisements and food stands selling ice cream, fruit, hot dogs and even pizza from a hat complete the sense of a bustling city street. Murdoch and Ogden often stroll along while horses and carriages amble by, and just as often find a crime scene or clue along the way.

The biggest bonus of this new outdoor space was allowing for more exterior scenes to be shot at night. Beautiful under simulated electric lamplight, Murdoch and Ogden were able to attend the theatre and kiss in a darkened laneway, while Crabtree and Grace could steal a few romantic moments after subduing a zombie horde. The world of *Murdoch* suddenly felt bigger and richer, and deeper inside our imaginations and our hearts.

But not everything can be shot on the backlot. *Murdoch Mysteries* does still travel around southern Ontario, and every so often across Canada (even once to England!), to help the intrepid detective solve his perplexing cases. The art department loves the challenge of taking a modern day streetscape or building and rewinding the clock more than one hundred years, to make it somewhere Murdoch would visit. Modern traffic signs, street numbers and neon store signs are covered with artfully placed shrubbery or period-perfect signage and decoration. Rarely does the production team find a street that can be shot its full length, and when that becomes a necessity, sometimes the art department needs a little virtual help.

## COMPUTER GENERATED IMAGES

Robert Crowther has been creating the period look on *Murdoch Mysteries* since the beginning, erasing telephone poles or electricity lines, and using greenscreens to extend streetscapes or create a landscape that production can't find in the real world.

Initially, CGI was introduced as a way to help broaden *Murdoch*'s world through the transitions – short sequences that play between scenes as a way of introducing or establishing the location in which the following scene will play.

The key transition needed from the very start was a short sequence to introduce Police Station No. 4. At the time there was no exterior for the police station and after

Main: *Crabtree and Murdoch spy a flying machine (601).*

Above and left: *Behind the scenes on the backlot (601).*

season 1, the front of the police station was not again used to shoot a scene until a new front was introduced in season 8. The production team found a location in Hamilton, the Hamilton Museum of Steam and Technology, which is a beautiful example of nineteenth century architecture, and an attached building with round windows and vaulted doors that could double for the exterior of the morgue. But the building was a bit small, considering the size of the police station set, and it lacked the imposing authority of a government building. Robert was called in to enhance the building, understanding that this would be a transition that would be used several times an episode. He set up a large greenscreen at the location, enabling him to add two more stories to what would be the front door, focusing first on the computer generated stone carving that read "Police Station No. 4", then sweeping down to the busy street below.

It wasn't just the police station that needed establishing. So too did many of the other settings for the varied places Murdoch would visit in the course of his investigations. But shooting an establishing shot every time the crew went on location was not always feasible. The idea was sparked to use vintage postcards, animated and brought to life. These postcard shots typically are used to place Murdoch and his colleagues in Toronto, but they have also been used to show that Murdoch is outside of Toronto, for example in New York City for his honeymoon.

To make these living postcards, Robert and his team first have to source or create digital versions of these old images. Most often these antique photographs are lying in archives, covered in dust and damaged by time, not yet preserved in a digital file. Robert then cleans the image, removing as much dust and debris as possible, then digitally fixes the broken parts of the image. Then he digitally paints over the image to colorize it. At that point he is ready to add in some actual people, background actors who have been previously filmed enacting scenes from daily life in front of a greenscreen.

One challenge was to ensure the correct perspective was in place. Angles of sidewalks and buildings required people to move along that same angle, though they had been filmed walking in a straight line. Another was to ensure the postcards were seasonally appropriate. The same postcard might be used in episode one of the season as in episode thirteen, and in the world of *Murdoch Mysteries* that would mean a change from spring to fall. Rob added in falling leaves instead of budding flowers, and although only on screen for a few seconds, this gives the audience a sense of time and place, even if just on a subconscious level. Detective Murdoch is all about the details when he solves a mystery, and the production team knows the details are just as important when building the fictional world in which those mysteries take place.

*The stages of creating an establisher postcard, from antique photograph (top left) to the image seen on screen (bottom; 305).*

## THE MUSIC

In the very early stages of development, the show knew what it would be on the page and on the screen, but not yet how to express that musically. Music can set a tone, heighten action, evoke emotion and is vital in creating the world we see on screen. Composer Rob Carli had worked on the TV movies of *Murdoch Mysteries*. When he was brought onto the television show, with its lighter tone and sensibility, initially he wasn't convinced it would work. However, tasked with finding a signature sound for the series, Rob immediately knew he wanted the sound to be modern and progressive, not the usual period drama string orchestra. He also wanted to evoke an industrial feeling as emblematic of the time period, rather than a romantic one, and to capture the mystery and the darkness. The tone of the show was to be lighter, but the crimes Murdoch was to solve would not be.

Rob used instruments of the time, percussive in nature, and experimented with metal, looking to echo the percussive sounds of the instruments. In so doing, he unwittingly complemented Cal Coons' directive for the show – more Jules Verne, less Dickens. Rob channeled the steampunk vibe of the new tone of the series, building it into the now iconic theme of *Murdoch Mysteries*.

Originally Rob presented three versions of the theme song. When he played them for the first time, Christina Jennings instantly chose the one we hear every week (*see left*). She knew instinctively that was Murdoch's theme, and she was right. A theme should tell you everything you need to know about the show that follows. Rob's theme has the steampunk elements, a shadow of darkness and mystery, yet with the promise of adventure and wit. All of the elements of *Murdoch Mysteries* captured in the one-minute opening sequence.

## ENTER THE CHARACTERS

With the story room in sync, the visual sense of the show established, and the music in place, *Murdoch Mysteries* had most of the elements for a hit television show. But the key to any series is to create a set of characters an audience can fall in love with. Characters in whom fans can invest their emotions and live vicariously through their adventures. Characters whom fans want to welcome into their homes every week, and in whom fans can find a part of themselves. Detective Murdoch, Dr Ogden, Constable Crabtree, Inspector Brackenreid and later Dr Grace, quickly became this set of characters. Well rounded, complex people played by talented actors, written with understanding and expertly costumed and set, the characters of *Murdoch Mysteries* blazed into being, and have since become members of our families, and a part of our daily lives.

# Detective
# WILLIAM MURDOCH

*"I'm not entirely sure I can envy a future where everyone wastes their lives staring at a screen watching made-up stories."*

# Detective
# WILLIAM MURDOCH

*Murdoch conducts research (601).*

The show is centred around our hero, Detective William Murdoch, a diligent policeman with a head for science and a nose for the truth. His unwavering dedication to solving his cases often places him in tricky situations, but he is unrelenting even in the face of danger. Murdoch is quiet, contemplative and private, but his actions always speak for him, and we see him as a complex man, endeavouring to make the world a better place, both through his scientific endeavours and by upholding the law. Initially Murdoch lives his life by the letter of the law, and by the strict moral code of the Catholic Church. Over the seasons Murdoch's view of life is challenged several times, and we see him begin to question the rules imposed by others, and develop his own moral code.

Murdoch and Crabtree investigate a kidnapping (511).

Murdoch spars with a captain who is hiding c

William Murdoch was born into a poor Catholic family in Nova Scotia. His father, Harry, was an alcoholic. His mother died when he was just a young boy. His sister Susannah left their unhappy home to join a convent. Murdoch also left, heading west, landing himself in a lumber camp in Northern Ontario. There he met a man who had been working as a constable in Toronto. It struck a chord with Murdoch and he decided to try his fortunes with the police.

Murdoch joined the Toronto Police as a constable, quickly working his way up to Acting Detective and finally the Detective of Police Station No. 4. His case-solving prowess is well known throughout the city, making an impression as far away as Parliament Hill, and his exploits make him famous enough to engender a small fan club, avidly searching the papers for the latest case he is working on. But his Catholic faith prevents him from further career advancement, it being a distinct disadvantage in the Protestant-run city. It is a testament to Murdoch's talents that he was able to rise even to detective, in itself a position of some prominence and with authority over the constables in his station house.

Fortunately for Toronto, it appears as though the majority of the murders committed in the city are in Station No. 4's division, encompassing the eastern portion of the city. Murdoch always solves the case, and only in a few very rare instances has the murderer eluded his grasp.

Murdoch is much appreciated, if not particularly understood, by the constables at Station No. 4. Not a stereotypical man of the lower classes, Murdoch will very rarely take a drink, and prefers to catch his criminals with his mind rather than his fists, but

# SUSANNAH MURDOCH

**SUSANNAH LEFT THE FAMILY HOME** at fourteen years of age to enter convent school and then chose to join a cloister in Montreal. She carried with her the anger over her mother's death and wanted nothing more than to escape it. Murdoch never expected he would see her again. When a murder investigation takes him to a Toronto convent, the last person he imagines as the Reverend Mother is his sister Susannah. He sees in her the person he might have been had he joined the priesthood as their mother had hoped. But Susannah can see Murdoch is exactly where and who he should be. Murdoch hopes to continue rebuilding their relationship when Susannah reveals, in one of the most heartbreaking scenes of the series, that she is ill, and will soon die, and she wishes to do so in the cloister in Montreal. We see the devastation and dashed dreams in Murdoch's eyes. But we also see him glad of the chance to say goodbye, and to have met his sister as the serene, devout and true-hearted woman he had hoped she would become.

*Susannah Murdoch (Michelle Nolden) (410).*

his tremendous success rate buys him the respect of his fellow coppers. If anything, the constables under him are somewhat in awe of his unconventional methods. Only Constable George Crabtree has the type of curious mind to learn and improve his own skills, making Murdoch rather proud in the process.

> *What people find appealing about William Murdoch is he's so righteous, he really is a good person and is really looking for the best in all situations.* Hélène Joy, *Dr Julia Ogden*

Murdoch lives at Mrs. Kitchen's boarding house on Ontario Street, close to the station house. He spends his time working, reading and giving confession. He is not one for a night at the pub or a vaudeville show. He prefers to read his books and journals, scientific or medical in nature, experiment or tinker with a new invention. With Ogden he will spend a night at the theatre, though only to please her. His idea of a good date involves touring exhibits of batteries, after all. Murdoch lives in his mind, and it is this mind that not only keeps Victorian Toronto safe, but also sets him apart from many other detectives, both fictional and otherwise, and makes him a hero to champion.

It is, of course, only fitting that Murdoch should find his one true love through his work. Prior to the series, he had been engaged to be married to another young woman, Liza Milner, who had died of consumption a year before we meet him in season 1. His dreams

*Murdoch visits Ogden in the morgue (206).*

# HARRY MURDOCH

**HARRY MURDOCH COULD NOT BE MORE DIFFERENT** from his son. A weak man, Harry is a slave to the bottle. Since Murdoch was a young boy and found his mother drowned in the shallow reeds near their modest home, he has blamed his father for her death. Carrying that anger around for so many years, Murdoch is not quite ready to revive a relationship with his father when he learns that, though Harry and his wife fought that fateful day, she tripped and fell, hitting her head, which caused the concussion that eventually led to her death. It was by all accounts an accident. Harry, having at least set that right with his son, moves out west. That doesn't stop him from embroiling Murdoch in yet another of his disasters, which puts Murdoch and Sergeant Jasper Linney together on a case. Neither being aware that the other is his half-brother. Ultimately, Murdoch's father may be a drunk, but he is not a bad man.

*Did You Know?*

Yannick's wife and all three of his daughters have appeared on the show. Two of them more than once.

*Above: Yannick shares a laugh with daughter Mikaela Bisson (Annie Cranston) on set (806).*

of a family dashed, he immerses himself in work, and finds himself drawn more and more to Dr Julia Ogden, the coroner in the city morgue. The more he works with her, the more they both realize how well suited they are for one another, despite their differences in social class and religion. If Murdoch were to believe in destiny, he would believe that everything in his life had led him to Ogden. And Ogden would believe the same.

However, that relationship takes years to come to fruition. In the meantime, Murdoch can't help but attract other female attention. Handsome, modest, pure of heart, a true gentleman by nature rather than by birth, with a passion that burns beneath a controlled exterior, and possessing of a certain nerdy charm, Murdoch could be the ultimate catch. But no matter how impossible their love may at times seem, he never truly wavers. Murdoch's heart is forever true to Julia Ogden.

*Murdoch and Sergeant Jasper Linney (Dylan Neal), newly discovered half-brothers, share a moment with their father Harry Murdoch (Stephen McHattie) (213).*

Supplement to the Toronto Fre

# SERGEANT JASPER LINNEY

MURDOCH IS CONFRONTED BY HIS MIRROR IMAGE – not in aspect, but in manner – when Sergeant Jasper Linney of the North West Mounted Police (the precursor to the world-famous Royal Canadian Mounted Police) inserts himself into a murder case in Toronto. Brackenreid and the constables are amazed at the similarities between the two exacting men, and enjoy watching Murdoch's annoyance at dealing with Jasper's idiosyncrasies, much the way they often have to deal with his. It's no surprise to anyone when Harry Murdoch becomes embroiled in the case, only to reveal that Jasper and Murdoch are, in fact, half-brothers. In true brotherly fashion, Jasper and Murdoch share an aptitude for science, rigging up a flash bang to subdue a gang of ruffians out to kill their newly discovered family. Thank goodness Jasper's place is in Canada's west – there is only room for one Murdoch per province, and Ontario is already spoken for!

**Did You Know?**

Yannick does not, has never, and will never wear mascara or any eye makeup. He was born with the kind of lashes every woman dreams of, lucky guy!

*Behind the scenes with Yannick and director John L'Ecuyer (112).*

# CASTING WILLIAM MURDOCH ✿✿✿✿✿✿✿✿✿✿✿✿✿✿✿✿✿✿✿✿✿✿✿✿✿✿✿✿✿✿✿✿✿✿✿

William Murdoch had already been brought to life in both books and television movies, but executive producer Cal Coons felt there was the potential to add another element to the character that had yet to be explored. William Murdoch should be a man of science.

What better way to capitalize on the Victorian era, the Industrial Revolution, and all of the scientific and technological breakthroughs of the nineteenth century than to put the show's protagonist right at the heart of it. Murdoch was to become a man of progress, with a scientific curiosity that would thrust him ahead of his peers. This aspect of his character became the key to the whole series, launching it into the future instead of keeping it mired in the past. Murdoch was to be a man ahead of his time, as much as a product of it.

So when it came to casting this new incarnation of William Murdoch, Cal was looking for some specific attributes. The actor playing Murdoch had to be handsome, of course, but he also needed to be vulnerable. He had to be able to embody the buttoned-up attitude of the period, and the restrained quiet of the character, but there needed to be a warmth, a compassion, and at the same time a resolve.

Enter Yannick Bisson. "I was scheduled for a first audition in early 2007," the actor recalls. "Just as I was starting to prep my material, the actors' union went on strike. The strike was for very good reasons, but man was I disappointed. I can't recall how long the strike lasted, but it was a few months, and I remember thinking that the Murdoch opportunity was probably gone.

"Then I got a call: 'Time to go in for Murdoch again!' So I went in and read. I remember there being lots of people there the first time. I was aware that there had been some *Murdoch* movies in the past and my agent arranged to get copies for me to reference.

"At the last minute I got a note sent through my agent that the series was to take a very different tone than the original movies and books. I was instructed not to reference anything that had been done to date. Hmm… 'Okay.'

"I read several times, I think three times," Bisson continues. "It was nerve-wracking. I kept thinking, 'Come on, let's do this already!!' Then I got word from my agent that the network was debating if they should cast older or younger for the role of William. So I thought, 'Great… Now who's this older guy?' I was then informed that I, in fact, was the 'older' one and that they had in mind a younger actor as well. Great!"

Luckily for us, the decision was made to keep Murdoch at his original age, Yannick was cast, and a Canadian icon was born.

Cal Coons was impressed with Yannick from his first audition. He had the vulnerability and the strength of character Cal was looking for. It became clear very early on that they had found William Murdoch. And once they had their Murdoch, everything else started to fall into place.

*Murdoch's office.*

# SETTING WILLIAM MURDOCH ✿✿✿✿✿✿✿✿✿✿✿✿✿✿✿✿✿✿✿✿✿✿✿✿✿✿✿✿✿✿✿✿✿✿✿✿✿✿✿✿✿✿✿✿✿✿✿

A key set for the series, Murdoch's office sees plenty of action: interviews with suspects and witnesses; his iconic chalkboard ruminations; discussions about the case at hand with Brackenreid, Crabtree, Ogden and Grace, and any variation thereof; romance and heartbreak with Ogden; Crabtree seeking advice; Brackenreid offering his (usually unsolicited) advice; experiments, research, evidence gathering, evidence analysis and so on. Much like Murdoch is the centre of the series, so Murdoch's office is the central set.

Murdoch's office has seen some changes over the years, but several things have remained the same. It is positioned so that Murdoch has a clear view over all of Station No. 4, straight through his windowed walls to the front entrance. From a story perspective, this allows Murdoch to always be aware of what is happening around him. From a practical perspective, the countless scenes shot in Murdoch's office have endless angles and background action to help keep the room looking fresh and interesting.

Murdoch's desk.

Murdoch presents a timeline for a murder (106).

Yannick Bisson and Ashley Leggat rehearse a scene in the interview room with director Sudz Sutherland (307).

When production designer Sandy Rybartas was thinking about the police station set as a whole, she knew she needed to be particularly mindful of the room that would essentially be Murdoch's home for the duration of the series. She and art director Armando Sgrignuoli made sure it was large enough to accommodate all the action it would be seeing. They even managed to eke out a tiny space on the side which could be curtained off as a private lab area, used most often for developing photographs, but also home to all sorts of hidden gadgets and research material Murdoch can access at will.

*[offi]ce set is my favourite. It looks the part... like the inner workings [of his] mind and also because it's where the whole story begins for me.*
*[Det]ective William Murdoch*

His office is not formal like Brackenreid's, instead it had to be able to function for Murdoch's investigative needs and to reflect the man who would be spending so much time in it. In the main space, it was key that Murdoch have a workspace for his various experiments. The large worktable was sourced from the CBC period collection. An old sewing table that tilts, it looked as though a great many crimes had been solved on it already, and it had the size and heft to hold up to all of Murdoch's chemicals and inventions.

In season 1, Sandy opted for a rolltop desk pushed against a wall for Murdoch to deal with his paperwork. Sandy felt that Murdoch needed a more private desk area, and that there would be more opportunities to film interviews in the office without a desk in between him and the witness or suspect. This was changed to the more conventional desk we associate with Murdoch in season 2, and has remained unaltered since.

To dress the set of Murdoch's office, Sandy and Armando looked for items that would reflect his more cerebral approach to detective work. Naturally there are a great many books lining shelves on almost every wall. His movable chalkboard is always in residence. Inventions – both those he built himself, and those of others Murdoch uses in his quest for the truth – sit on any available surface. But the small items are the ones that reveal Murdoch the man. A chess board was placed in the corner by the door. Sometimes used in the recreation of a crime scene, and usually by Crabtree at that, the chess set alludes to Murdoch's creative mind and intellectual strategy. Similar touches line the walls and shelves, all hinting at the unique mind of Murdoch. Set dressing is a composition of elements that evoke the spirit of what the show is attempting to portray, and in Murdoch's office we feel his spirit of inquisitiveness and uniqueness, and believe

# DRESSING WILLIAM MURDOCH

Costume designer Alex Reda knew that his choices for Murdoch would set a tone for the character, so he turned to Murdoch's backstory for help. Murdoch's religious upbringing was central to Alex's approach to the character, as was his social standing.

A police detective in Victorian Toronto did not earn a high wage. Murdoch's wardrobe had to be simple, modest, yet professional. Alex kept the colour palette somber and serious, in keeping with Murdoch's line of work. Murdoch has several suits, of varying dark shades, and though he wears different suits throughout an episode, Alex made it a point to have them look so similar as to be almost indistinguishable. Murdoch himself would not be preoccupied with fashion, rather with cleanliness and neatness, and his suits reflect his sense of propriety. Only his tie would be noticeably different as one day changes to the next in the course of any given episode.

Yannick truly appreciates the beautiful suits, all made to measure and impeccably tailored. After eight seasons Murdoch's wardrobe consists of around fifteen suits, many white shirts and several ties, but Yannick jokes that although the suits are all different, once onscreen, even he struggles to see anything more distinctive than just another dark suit.

*Alex Reda and his team have done an amazing job of dressing us all on the show for all eight years.*

Yannick Bisson, *Detective William Murdoch*

`MURDOCH`
SEASON I

*Right: Alex Reda's costume design for one of Murdoch's work suits.*

The key to Murdoch's look, though – and the item of clothing that has become his visual signature – was finding the right hat. The hat would always be with him, and would therefore become an integral part of his character. Alex tried a bowler hat first, but it wasn't quite right; it didn't seem smart or distinctive enough for Murdoch's character. The shape also didn't quite flatter Yannick's classic features. So Alex turned to a homburg. The homburg has a more modern feel to it, and was a less popular shape amongst the working classes. Thus, Murdoch's hat was chosen, and it has become not only the symbol for his character, but also of the entire series.

*Dr Iris Bajjali (Athena Karkanis) and Murdoch analyze the sarcophagus (503).*

## THE INVENTIONS OF WILLIAM MURDOCH

Where Murdoch truly shines is in his unique application of Victorian science and technology to his crime solving. Science is this great detective's superpower, and his use of the discoveries of the age is always creative and always brings results. At the turn of the nineteenth century, new forensic techniques were still only in the early stages of being adopted by police forces worldwide. Murdoch, in his quest for knowledge, is always at the forefront of these advances, and often ahead of them. As writer Paul Aitken explains, if the technology already existed, there is no reason why Murdoch can't use that technology in tandem with another separate technology to create whatever it is he

**Did You Know?**

Property master Craig Grant makes an appearance in full costume in the background of an episode at least once a season.

*Above: Murdoch and Crabtree at the Invention Convention (509).*

*Main: Murdoch uses his night vision goggles to escape a possible attack (209).*

*Craig Grant as an inventor at the convention (509).*

needs. The writers are very conscious of adapting modern crime-solving techniques within the boundaries of Victorian capabilities, but also enjoy giving Murdoch's genius the freedom to shine.

While the writers can put anything they like on the page, it's up to property master Craig Grant to realize their ideas in a way that is believable for the time period, functions for the story, and looks like something Murdoch himself could have made in his office. The inventions onscreen look deceptively easy, but they are quite the opposite. Feats of engineering and ingenuity, Craig has made some incredible props on Murdoch's behalf.

Craig typically has two weeks to design, source and build whatever invention the next script calls for. In the early seasons, he would build most of the inventions himself, by hand, using mainly the same tools Murdoch would have had at his disposal. Most of Murdoch's gadgets are cobbled together from found objects, different Victorian-era items Craig finds at flea markets or online, that he then repurposes to create the right look for a Victorian invention, with the homemade quality that makes it believable as Murdoch's own creation.

A favourite example of this is Murdoch's circumscope – a device he uses to see over a wall while remaining hidden behind it – its original incarnation appearing in season 1 and made from various materials, including Brackenreid's missing opera glasses. Then, while on his honeymoon with Ogden in season 8, Murdoch improves on this design. He successfully creates an extended version of his original circumscope that can see into the room above his own, taking advantage of the bathroom pipes and Ogden's cosmetic mirrors to build it.

*Murdoch takes a close look at the evidence (102).*

# A FEW NOTABLE INVENTIONS

- THE PNEUMOGRAPH or TRUTHIZER (named by Crabtree in season 5): An ahead of-its-time lie detector used to great advantage, though not very marketable in the end.
- THE INDUCTION BALANCING MACHINE: A metal detecto that requires a bicycle to be pedalled (by Brackenreid) to power it.
- THE SCRUTINY CAMERA: An automatic surveillance camera used to trap all kinds of villians over the seasons.
- THE WEAPONIZED CAPACITOR: A taser used to bring down criminals without the use of lethal force.

*Murdoch tests the truthizer (108).*

*Weaponized capacitor (818).*

Side

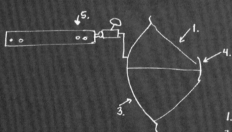

1. Brass Rod
2. Brass Flat
3. Para Mirror
4. Convex Mirror
5. Headband

Front

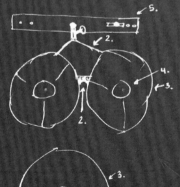

Single Mirror

Hole in Centre of Disk.

*Night vision goggles (209).*

*Murdoch and Crabtree test out Murdoch's new circumscope (110).*

Even when not scripted, Craig will stick with household objects in his designs. In season 2, Murdoch builds a model of a bank vault to determine how the killer got inside. Craig built that model himself, exactly as Murdoch would have, using only materials Murdoch would have had lying around. In this way, the inventions we see have an authenticity. Not shiny and glossy, not perfect reproductions of their real-life modern counterparts, the props that Craig builds enhance the fictional world in which they work.

Much like all of the props used on the show, Murdoch's inventions are true to the time and, most importantly, true to the man who is meant to have made them.

## SCORING WILLIAM MURDOCH

Not every character on the show has a specific musical theme, but Detective Murdoch has at least three.

The majority of the action on *Murdoch Mysteries* is in Murdoch's head, and the music is there to take it from a strictly cerebral pursuit to that of heart-pumping action. As it's important that the music doesn't become too slow, Rob Carli uses modern rhythms with significant backbeat to keep tempos up and pulses pounding.

Playing off of the main theme of the show, Murdoch's themes are all variations of the same exploration between major and minor chords. There is a theme to accompany Murdoch's mind as he puzzles out a question – his thinking music. There is a theme to accompany Murdoch as he furiously cycles to apprehend a murderer – his chasing music. There is also a theme to accompany Murdoch's visualisations wherein he solves a case – his vision music. Each of these themes is distinct yet similar. They all fully utilise the tone of mystery and ingenuity that pervades the music throughout, and clue the audience in to what we are watching, what Murdoch is thinking, and what he is attempting to do in any given scene.

## MAKING MURDOCH'S VISIONS

Referred to as "Murdoch Visions" in the scripts, these are the moments in which Murdoch enters a scene inside his head and imagines the sequence of events, having not been there himself, to solve the case at hand. In the early seasons, these were used quite frequently, as a glimpse into the inner workings of Murdoch's unique mind. He can pull together all of the facts in his head, and lay them out in front of him, entering the frame as an observer in his own recreation of the crime.

In season 1, the visions were used frequently and to great effect, a stylistic hallmark of the show. Cal Coons and Jim Jeffrey, the director of photography, brainstormed different ways of creating a visual style that would be specific to the visions, helping the audience to understand that we are transitioning into Murdoch's mind. The decision was to begin a vision with a zoom into Murdoch's eyes, transporting us directly into his brain. The vision itself would be filmed on a different camera, so that it would look quite distinct from the regular onscreen action.

Jim used a Bell and Howell 16mm camera from the 1940s to achieve this. Hand cranked with a small, off centre viewfinder, Jim himself would operate the camera during the filming of the visions, to ensure they captured everything they needed. He employed a trick wherein the film would be cranked forward, then backwards onto itself, double printing the film with the action in front of him. This created a double image that gave Murdoch's visions an almost ethereal, otherworldly effect.

As the seasons went on and film cameras fell out of favour, it became more and more difficult for the production team to find labs that could develop the 16mm film. Finally in season 7, Jim's Bell and Howell broke, and the last film lab in Canada closed down. It was a sign. The Murdoch Visions would have to change.

Jim took to using a Nikon still camera. By attaching a "lens baby" (a bellows-type lens that resembles a small accordion which, when moved around distorts the image, focussed on one side and blurred on the other) Jim was able to create a new visual style that still achieved the same goal – to keep Murdoch's vision distinct from the main shooting style. As Murdoch's style of detecting has evolved over the years, so too have the cameras that capture it.

*Murdoch Visions.*

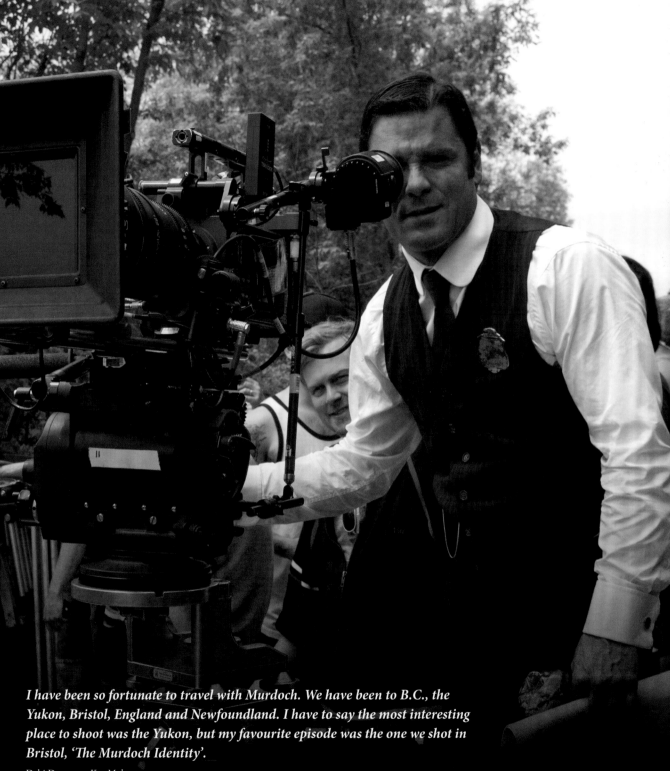

*I have been so fortunate to travel with Murdoch. We have been to B.C., the Yukon, Bristol, England and Newfoundland. I have to say the most interesting place to shoot was the Yukon, but my favourite episode was the one we shot in Bristol, 'The Murdoch Identity'.*

Debi Drennan, *Key Makeup*

*Director Yannick Bisson prepares his next shot on location at the South Simcoe Railway in Tottenham (803).*

# Doctor
# JULIA OGDEN

*"We're all animals, William, behaving as nature intended. If God didn't want us to express our desires, then why did he give us these desires in the first place."*

*Ogden and Murdoch inspect the corpse of Constable Cooper (Martin Happer) (302).*

# *Doctor* JULIA OGDEN

Dr Julia Ogden is a woman able to work in a man's world, in a constant battle with the establishment. Love interest to Murdoch, she stands apart from women of the time with her progressive views and disregard for convention. A role model and an inspiration, not only to the women of the fictional world of *Murdoch Mysteries*, but to the modern women who watch Ogden's constant struggle on their screens each week.

Born in Toronto, Ogden's mother died when she was just a young girl. She and her sister, Ruby Ogden, were left to their father to raise. Not one to show his emotions, Dr Lionel Ogden hoped to raise them as proper gentlewomen. But neither of them was destined for a life of social convention.

*Ogden takes notes in her lab (105).*

*Ogden tells Brackenreid that John Tucker was shot prior to the blast (112).*

# RUBY OGDEN

Julia Ogden is a free spirit in private, but her younger sister Ruby has no qualms about splashing her own unconventional lifestyle across the pages of newspapers around the world. A journalist with a nose for the story behind the story, Ruby has a habit of attaching herself to interesting men, both romantically and professionally, to get deeper into the story she is reporting. She first appears as an assistant on stage to Harry Houdini, much to Ogden's embarrassment. Ruby then becomes the companion of H.G. Wells, who in turn is entranced by the elder Ogden sister on his visit to Toronto.

Beautiful and charismatic, Ruby is a notorious flirt. Where Ogden uses wit and intelligence to achieve what she wants, Ruby uses her feminine wiles. She and her sister share a competitive spirit, and once Ruby spots her sister's obvious affection for Murdoch, Ruby wastes no time in attempting to win him over for herself, only succeeding in making Murdoch extremely uncomfortable and Ogden extremely annoyed. Some time spent with George Crabtree appears to shift the focus of her interest, however, and though the two never do court, the potential pairing of Ruby and George still has many supporters.

Ruby has more in common with her sister than she cares to admit. Forced to report her stories under a male nom de plume, "Rupert Olsen," Ruby knows all too well the obstacles in the way of a woman's success in the world. She admires her sister, and loves her, but Ruby is frustrated at her sister's cowardice when it comes to William Murdoch. Ruby herself has never found true love, only casual dalliances. She is the only one who tells Ogden not to squander it. And when Murdoch and Ogden finally do get married, Ruby is overjoyed, though she isn't able to be there to see it for herself.

Julia Ogden chose to become a doctor and follow in her father's footsteps. She was never deterred by her gender. There were a handful of women working as doctors in Canada, but it was still uncommon for women to become professionals in any capacity. It would not be easy, but Ogden was never a woman to shrink from a challenge. She enrolled in Bishop's University, where she would have been a contemporary of Octavia Grace Ritchie, the first woman to graduate from medical school in Quebec in 1891.

Her trailblazing spirit continued as she returned to Toronto and applied for a position at the city morgue. Her talent won over her gender, and she was appointed city coroner, where she would meet Detective William Murdoch, and a hesitant but deep friendship began to develop.

Publicly, Ogden comports herself with all of the social graces with which she was raised. Hélène Joy admires Ogden's grace and poise. Ogden is a modern woman with a classic education, and she equally shuns and embraces the class into which she was born. She attends the opera, charity balls, fine restaurants and other such social events, where she fits right in, but finds the exclusivity of the rowing club and the snobbery of her class insufferable. Her modern views on medicine and women's rights do have a tendency to rub some of the old establishment the wrong way, and she naughtily delights in their discomfort. During her marriage to Dr Darcy Garland in season 5, Ogden would struggle to contain her opinions and would inevitably embarrass Darcy in the presence of his superiors, especially with regard to her controversial opinions on contraception. But she is never blind to the effect of her words. She may overstep at times, but she is always passionate about the cause at hand, and usually frustrated by the rigid and unyielding opposition put before her.

Privately, however, Ogden is a true free spirit. She once went skinny dipping, had relations with a man well before marriage, and chose to be the subject of a highly illegal and dangerous treatment to end a pregnancy. Not something she chose to do lightly, she still made her own choice, at a time when the choice did not exist for women. This controversial decision was not without consequence however. Ogden was told she would not be able to have children again, her friend Dr Isaac Tash was aggressively investigated for conducting these illegal procedures, and most calamitous of all, in season 2 it forced Ogden and Murdoch to part ways, the first of many misunderstandings and poor decisions that would keep them apart for many years to come.

The series introduces Ogden as Murdoch's friend and colleague, as an integral part of his investigations, and as an independent, intelligent and talented woman. She is Murdoch's social better, but his intellectual equal. A character with a story of her own to tell, she is more than just Murdoch's true love. She is a scientist, an activist, a trailblazer and an adventurer.

*Murdoch shares his theory about an assassination attempt with Ogden (502).*

*Ogden takes aim (608).*

*Dr Darcy Garland (Jonathan Watton) and Ogden marry (413).*

# DARCY GARLAND

WHEN OGDEN DECIDES TO LEAVE THE MORGUE, accepting a position at the Buffalo Children's Hospital, her desire to put all things Toronto behind her sends her straight into the arms of Dr Darcy Garland. A good man from a good family, Darcy is exactly the kind of man Ogden should marry. Educated, wealthy, upper class, and besotted with her, Darcy's proposal of marriage is hard for Ogden to resist. He comes at just the right time. Ogden and Murdoch are over, she feels she must move on with her life and Darcy provides the path. She could not have known how he would change.

Though he initially appears to enjoy and even agree with Ogden's progressive viewpoints on both medicine and the world, once married he becomes less the enchanted suitor and more the chagrined Victorian husband. Ogden sets up her private practice in their house in Toronto, and though Darcy doesn't complain, he begins to subtly provoke her to stop her controversial clinic and fall back in line with the establishment. When subtlety doesn't work, Darcy outright tells her to stop. She is putting his position and reputation in jeopardy with her foolhardy schemes. It's difficult to judge Darcy. He gives up his life in Buffalo and moves away from his family to be with Ogden. He does love her. He can't help that his breeding and ambition incline him to behave as a product of the time. He is not the right man for Ogden, as everyone but he knows, and he ultimately pays for this ignorance with his life.

### Did You Know?

There was a Facebook page dedicated to the death of Darcy Garland. A group of fans willed his death and were no doubt thrilled to see it happen on screen!

*Above: Ogden uses her x-ray machine on Jeremiah Fuller (Grant Nickalls), as Grace looks on (705).*

*Main: Ogden checks the body of Claude Benoit (113).*

# The Careers of
## JULIA OGDEN

Acareer woman was an unusual occurrence in Victorian Toronto. There were plenty of young women in the city who worked in all sorts of capacities, but most of that work didn't qualify as a career, and middle class women would stop working once married to keep house and raise families. Upper class women like Ogden typically would not work at all, but spend their days educating themselves in music and art, or volunteering with charities. Ogden did not need to work. She chose to be independent and forge her own path. A path with many twists and turns.

## THE MORGUE

Ogden begins her working life in the city morgue of Toronto. She excels at deciphering the clues a body leaves behind, and her compassion for the victims is what drives her to discover their killers. Creative in her methodology, Ogden is never shy about trying a new device or experiment to help uncover the truth. From "borrowing" a brand new X-ray machine from the hospital to using new foodstuff Jell-O to determine the murder weapon, Ogden is always full of surprises.

The morgue surprises her as well. When a dead body rises from the morgue table in season 3's 'Hangman', Ogden is rightfully shaken – one of the very few times we see her lose her composure. Though more often it is a place of solitude, where Ogden can be alone with her science and her thoughts, and whatever risqué music is currently striking her fancy.

Her decision to leave the morgue is not easy. At first she takes a position at the children's hospital in Buffalo. She tells Murdoch it's because she needs to use her medical training to help heal those who still have a chance to live. But we all know Ogden is running away from heartbreak, as she and Murdoch have yet to openly move past her inability to have children.

When she returns to the morgue in season 4, engaged to Darcy, we watch as she and Murdoch both suffer to stifle their feelings, engrossing themselves in the case at hand. By the beginning of season 5, Ogden is married. She knows she can't continue working so closely with Murdoch. She leaves the morgue yet again, but this time it's for good.

*Ogden in jail for promoting contraception (507).*

*Ogden oversees Sarah Bosen's (Melissa Hood) phobia treatment (706).*

*Eva Pearce (Daiva Johnston-Zalnieriunas), Ogden, Hannah (Tara Nicodemo) and*

## PRIVATE PRACTICE ✦✦✦✦✦✦✦✦✦✦✦✦✦✦✦✦✦✦✦✦✦✦✦✦✦✦✦✦✦✦✦✦✦✦✦✦✦✦✦✦✦✦✦✦

Ogden, now married, opens a women's clinic in her stately home. She quickly finds that poor women are overburdened with children, and the laws of the day are not on her side. A woman is not legally allowed to terminate a pregnancy, something Ogden knows only too well, and attempting to prevent a pregnancy is just as unlawful. Ogden has found her new crusade. She begins teaching contraception in her clinic, in her own house, and is discovered and thrown in jail. Undeterred, Ogden continues her private practice at her own peril. It is one of the factors in the ultimate demise of her marriage to Darcy, though as we all know, Ogden's wilfulness is only a symptom of the larger reason. Her heart will always belong to someone else.

## PSYCHIATRY ✦✦✦✦✦✦✦✦✦✦✦✦✦✦✦✦✦✦✦✦✦✦✦✦✦✦✦✦✦✦✦✦✦✦✦✦✦✦✦✦✦✦✦✦✦✦✦✦✦✦

Ogden's true heart is shown to her when she is kidnapped by über-villain James Gillies, in his never-ending quest to torment Detective Murdoch. Upon her rescue, she is subject to bad dreams, which are only finally eradicated by a form of electro-shock treatment administered by the friendly psychiatrist Dr Roberts. Intrigued by the effectiveness of the cure, and even more by the nightmares that necessitated it, Ogden finds herself drawn toward the workings of the mind. Psychiatry at the turn of the nineteenth century was still considered by the wider medical community as quackery, but new theories and tests were beginning to convince more and more people of its veracity as a field of study and treatment. Ogden's entry into psychiatry coincides with a time when some institutions, including the Provincial Lunatic Asylum, were beginning to lean towards gentler, more humane practices, employing techniques like art therapy instead of, though sometimes in addition to, the more torturous practices of old.

The tragic demise of Dr Roberts leaves a place open at the Provincial Lunatic Asylum, which Ogden seizes, carving out a place for herself countering the misdiagnosis and general societal misunderstanding of women. Coinciding with the death of her marriage, Ogden can see a future in this new endeavour. Not only will she be braving a new frontier, that of the mind, but she will be once again able to help Murdoch with his work. It seems an ideal prospect to Ogden, on the eve of a new century, with a new career and a new chance at the life she's always wanted right in front of her.

## SUFFRAGE ✦✦✦✦✦✦✦✦✦✦✦✦✦✦✦✦✦✦✦✦✦✦✦✦✦✦✦✦✦✦✦✦✦✦✦✦✦✦✦✦✦✦✦✦✦✦

Content in her work as a psychiatrist, and happy at last in her marriage to Murdoch, Ogden's adventurous and progressive spirit finds itself swept up in the fight for women's suffrage. Approached to run in a provincial election, Ogden declines for the sake of Murdoch's career. She may be ahead of the times, but the men who employ her husband are not, and anyway she doesn't need the spotlight, just the cause. So she campaigns instead for Margaret Haile, the first woman to run for public office in all of the British Empire, if not the world, and finds renewed vigour in the fight for how she has lived her life. Not all women had the privilege to challenge social norms. Ogden is living proof of what a Victorian woman could achieve, and a reminder to women today of the rights we take for granted, and the inequality that still exists despite them.

*Rob Carli's score for the suffragette protest (801).*

*Filming the suffragette protest on location at Queen's Park (801).*

*Ogden, Grace, Kathleen King (Trenna Keating) and Margaret Haile (Nicole Underhay) in the courtroom (802).*

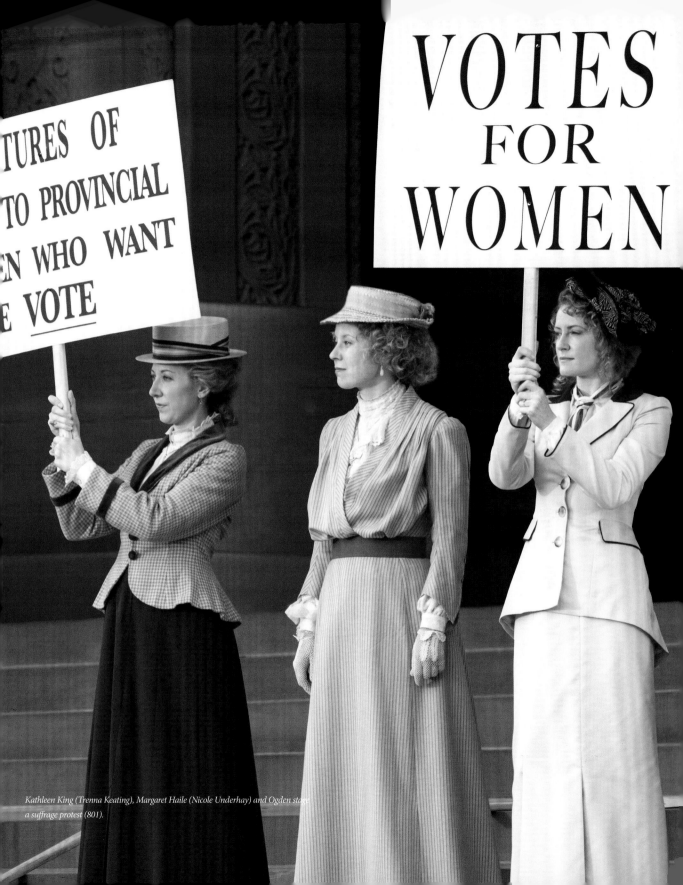

*Kathleen King (Trenna Keating), Margaret Haile (Nicole Underhay) and Ogden stage*
*a suffrage protest (801).*

## CASTING JULIA OGDEN ❁❁❁❁❁❁❁❁❁❁❁❁❁❁❁❁❁❁❁❁❁❁❁❁❁❁❁❁❁❁❁❁❁❁❁❁❁❁❁❁❁❁❁

During its development, the producers knew that the casting of Dr Ogden would be key to the success of the series. In the first four seasons, she was the only female regular cast member. She needed to have a classic look but a contemporary attitude. She needed to wear the clothes and exude the era, believable as a woman born and raised during the reign of Queen Victoria. She had to carry herself as a woman of good breeding and wealth, but still have an edge, a curiosity, and light behind her eyes. She had to be attractive, in an intelligent, restrained way. In short, Julia Ogden had to be the kind of woman William Murdoch would fall in love with, and the kind of woman we would want for him.

Cal Coons recalls how Hélène Joy's classical bearing and expressive eyes had put her firmly on the radar in the early days of casting. She had already appeared in one of the television movies of *Murdoch Mysteries*, and had proven she could emulate a Victorian woman.

Hélène remembers being told about the role by Maureen Jennings, who had loved the work Hélène had done in the television movie. But then she heard the producers had decided to go much younger with the role, and that she would be out of the running. So when the call came from her agent, she was pleasantly surprised. She was called in for the last round of auditions, up against a handful of other candidates. Hélène recalls purposely dressing modestly, with a longer skirt and her hair up, to try and capture the spirit of the era for her audition. When she was called back, she was asked to come in looking as natural as possible. She wore a contemporary satin dress and, though she can't recall why, it seemed to have been a good choice. She won the role and Julia Ogden was born.

Cal recalls auditioning Hélène with Yannick for the first time. He could feel their chemistry instantly, and could see Ogden in Hélène. It's important for a writer to see what an actor brings to a role, and in Hélène he could see how to write for the way she embodied the spirit of Julia Ogden. He had written a scene specifically for casting purposes that was never filmed, in the context of the mystery that would become the season 1 episode 'Still Waters'. The scene involved Murdoch and Ogden on a wharf following a blood trail. Cal saw both Yannick and Hélène inherently understand what he was going for as they crawled around on the floor following the imaginary blood. They were almost as interested in the blood trail as they were in each other, and the awkwardness of their obvious feelings for one another shone through the words and brought their relationship instantly to life.

*Script pages for the audition scene (top) and a moment from the episode it became, 'Still Waters' (108).*

EXT. ROWING CLUB - DAY

Murdoch is examining a dock when Ogden approaches.

                    OGDEN
          I'm sorry about that.

                    MURDOCH
          No, no.  Perfectly fine.

                    OGDEN
          Dr. Tash and I haven't seen one
          another in some time and --

                    MURDOCH
               (changing the subject)
          My men are going over every inch of
          the dock, but no sign of blood so
          far.

                    OGDEN
          Well, there should be some, given
          the laceration on the foot.

                    MURDOCH
          Unless he was cut in the water.

                    OGDEN
          Yes, of course, that's possible.

                    MURDOCH
          I'm convinced there must be some
          trace.

Murdoch gets onto his hands and knees and begins to examine
the dock.  Ogden drops to her knees and joins him.  They
crawl along.

                    OGDEN
          Let me help you.

                    MURDOCH
          I had no idea you were a member here.

                    OGDEN
          My family is.  Have been for some
          time.  I don't really visit the club
          much anymore.

                    MURDOCH
          No?  I would think it would be most
          engaging.

                    OGDEN
          I find it tiresome.

                    MURDOCH
          And Dr. Tash?  You didn't seem to
          find him tiresome.

Ogden shoots Murdoch a look.  Jealousy?  Murdoch stops, pulls
out a tweezer and vial from his jacket.

                    OGDEN
          As I said, he's an old friend.

                    MURDOCH
          I see.
               (lifts the tweezer)
          Glass shard.

                    OGDEN
          I would think larger than that to
          cause the cut.

Murdoch continues his search.

                    MURDOCH
          Did you and Dr. Tash attend medical
          school together?

                    OGDEN
          I must say, you seem quite curious
          about Dr. Tash.

                    MURDOCH
          Simply making conversation.

                    OGDEN
          I would have thought probing a more
          accurate description.

FANTASY -- Murdoch suddenly leans forward and kisses Ogden.

                    OGDEN (CONT'D)
          William.

REALITY -- Murdoch stares at Ogden, never having kissed her.

                    OGDEN (CONT'D)
          William?  Is there something you'd
          like to ask me?

                    MURDOCH
          Uh, yes, uh, how large of a shard
          might we be looking for?

Ogden nods, slightly disappointed.

# Setting
## JULIA OGDEN

✦✦✦✦✦✦✦✦✦✦✦✦✦✦✦✦✦✦✦✦✦✦✦✦✦✦✦✦✦✦

*Filming Ogden examining a victim (102).*

*Murdoch shows Ogden a telephonic probe (104).*

## THE MORGUE ✦✦✦✦✦✦✦✦✦✦✦✦✦✦✦✦✦✦✦✦✦✦✦✦✦✦✦✦✦✦✦✦✦✦✦✦✦✦✦✦✦✦✦✦✦✦✦✦✦✦✦✦✦✦

During pre-production, the morgue was defined as a cold, clinical place. To make it Ogden's own, the art department added a few personal touches. Her medical certificates hang on the wall beside Ogden's desk, showing her credentials with pride, and no small degree of satisfaction, for anyone who enters the morgue to see. Ogden's goldfish in the early seasons was there to counterbalance the overwhelming atmosphere of death. Ogden may be surrounded by death, but she is very much alive. Her compassion and warmth are evident in the way she cares for the living while working on the dead.

The Edison phonograph was also a key character point for Ogden. Only a woman of confidence and some daring would play jaunty popular tunes while performing post-mortem examinations. Other feminine touches dot the raised areas surrounding the examination table, though the examination area itself is spartan and spotless, always ready for the next challenge. Not afraid to get her hands dirty, Ogden uses every space available when conducting her work. She is a professional, and the morgue reflects exactly that.

*I have a weakness for the morgue. It is such a beautiful set.*

Hélène Joy, *Dr Julia Ogden*

*Murdoch and Ogden discuss a case (502).*

Above: *Ogden shows Sir Arthur Conan Doyle (Geraint Wyn Davies) one of her tools of the trade (104).*

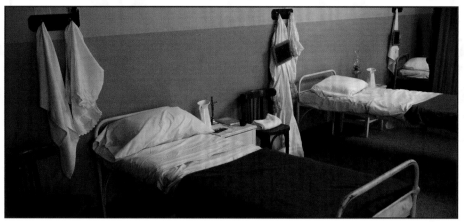

*An asylum ward.*

## THE ASYLUM ✿✿✿✿✿✿✿✿✿✿✿✿✿✿✿✿✿✿✿✿✿✿✿✿✿✿✿✿✿✿✿✿✿✿✿✿✿✿✿✿✿✿✿✿✿✿✿✿

When Ogden moves to work at the asylum, production designer Sandy Kybartas was given the opportunity to design another new standing set. It needed to reflect both Ogden's approach to psychiatry and the evolution of her character by season 6, as well as work for all of the practical concerns of filming. Ogden's office was to be modern and bright, quite unlike our idea of a Victorian asylum. Ogden would be ushering in a new, more compassionate age of psychiatry, and her office would need to reflect that approach. With the doctor having just returned from Europe, where she studied with Sigmund Freud (1856-1939) – commonly known as the father of psychoanalysis – Sandy looked to incorporate a European flavour into Ogden's new workplace. She chose muted, calming colours and rich cozy fabrics like velvet to create a warm and inviting atmosphere for Ogden's patients. A roll top desk set against the wall kept Ogden's correspondence and reports private, while keeping the room open and intimate for any visitors. Sandy and art director Armando wanted to reflect Ogden's more humane approach to her patients with art and plants. An avant-garde painting on an easel demonstrates this forward-thinking attitude to her work and the European influence of her recent studies abroad. The office was to convey a certain boldness, which is inherently Ogden's character, but also a kindness and generosity emblematic of her psychiatric style.

Through the wall of windows Ogden can keep an eye on her patients. In charge of the female ward, whenever we see Ogden in her office we also see women in their beds or wheelchairs, not in distress but in calm repose under Ogden's care. This depth of field enriches the scenes filmed in Ogden's office, as we get a sense of the work she is doing off camera and outside of Murdoch's cases.

*Ogden in her office in the asylum (607).*

There are some things that stayed constant between Ogden's morgue and Ogden's office. Sharp-eyed viewers will spot the same phrenology head and the same phonograph that Ogden kept over the years. She has grown and changed, but her love of science and music have only grown with her.

## DRESSING JULIA OGDEN

One aspect of *Murdoch Mysteries* that viewers have often noted is the frequency with which the women rotate their pieces of clothing. As was true then, even women of the upper classes had a limited number of outfits, and would invariably wear the same clothing in various combinations more than once a week. Alex Reda used this to his advantage when designing Ogden's beautiful and unique wardrobe. Many pieces are reused and recut over the seasons to fit new fashions or new requirements, as would have happened in Victorian times. It may be budget-friendly, but it also feels authentic and helps draw the viewers in to the era in which Ogden lives.

In the early seasons, while Ogden was working in the morgue, Alex had to keep practicality in mind. However, as there were very few women working in medicine at the time, and likely none in a morgue, Alex had virtually no photographic references to work with. This made dressing Ogden a challenge, but also gave him freedom to create her clothing based on the character, rather than her real-life historical counterparts. Ogden could tow the line between fashionable and practical. Working in a profession dominated by men where everything would be black and white, Alex chose to feature strong colours in Ogden's clothing – a conscious attempt to infuse her with light while surrounded by the macabre.

Nevertheless, her everyday clothing needed to be professional. A woman working in a man's world would wear a woman's version of men's clothing. Smart suits with crisp blouses, waistcoats with neckties topped with unisex boater hats helped give her a no-nonsense and capable look. Alex then balanced the severity of this masculinity of form by using feminine fabrics in his designs. He also slightly reduced the shape of her skirt to create a more fluid silhouette to differentiate her from other women of the day. And, in keeping with Ogden's nonconformist attitude, Alex chose to roll up her sleeves and lower her necklines, boldly demonstrating her free spirit and strength in such a conservative profession and world.

Hélène Joy has always been particularly enamoured of a navy blue suit with a perfectly cut waistcoat. It felt very smart-looking to her and helped her feel confident and capable, just like Ogden, every time she put it on.

*Below: Two Alex Reda costume designs for Ogden.*

*Two more Alex Reda designs*

With the changes in Ogden's careers, so her wardrobe also changed. Free of the morgue, Alex could introduce more feminine elements into her clothing. Lace, flounced sleeves and softer colours were all used more frequently. Along with these changes came changes in fashion, as the show moved from the Victorian to the Edwardian eras. Ogden's necklines began to creep back up, her clothes became a little softer and the colours more muted, with more streamlined silhouettes and more delicate fabrics.

Every so often Alex has the chance to dress Ogden in evening wear, enjoying the opportunity to be a bit more scandalous. Showing off Ogden's bare arms and accentuating her bust, creating a sexy yet romantic look that could not happen in her day clothing. From a crime scene in season 1 to the Dinosaur Ball of season 3, to the New Year's Policeman's Ball of season 5, Alex has designed some truly beautiful gowns.

Since Ogden's marriage to Murdoch early in season 8, the audience has been privy to some of the couple's more intimate moments behind closed doors. Ogden's true-to-the-period underclothing was on full display before her wedding, and we were treated to a glimpse of the number of layers a woman would have worn under her already substantial dresses. Alex used authentic and natural fabrics like silk and cotton to create these undergarments. They, as well as all the rest of Ogden's clothing, are designed by him, then patterned and hand cut, then expertly sewn, fitted, adjusted and re-sewn until each item fits Hélène like a glove. Alex has a team of seamstresses and cutters to help him with his original designs. Ogden is dressed to perfection because of Alex and his team, who manage to recreate an era and satisfy the audience's desire for beauty, balancing out the crime and murder she must deal with every week.

# *Constable*
# GEORGE CRABTREE

*"That's a fantastic idea! I've never got the hang of slicing a piece of bread, sir... Sliced bread would be the greatest thing since... since..."*

*Crabtree arrives at a crime scene (202).*

*Brackenreid, Murdoch and Crabtree team up to investigate a new case (210).*

## Constable
# GEORGE CRABTREE

George Crabtree, born in Toronto but raised in Newfoundland, is Murdoch's right hand man. A man with a generous heart and an indefatigable spirit, Crabtree is a fan favourite. He is fiercely loyal, and holds both Murdoch and Brackenreid in high esteem. His dream is to be as good a copper as Murdoch, and he spends most of his time at work endeavouring to live up to that very high standard.

Crabtree has a very unusual provenance. Born in Toronto to poor parents, he was left on the doorstep of a church while just a baby. He was raised by the good Reverend, with significant help from his often-referenced "Aunts", in Newfoundland, but returned to Toronto as a young man to join the police and make his way in life.

Penny Ranton (Brianna Bisson, Yannick Bisson's daughter) (309).

**COUSIN PENNY**

CRABTREE IS VISITED BY HIS COUSIN in season 3, and we see his brotherly side come to the fore. Sixteen-year-old Penny is only interested in being close to her seventeen-year-old sweetheart, with every intention to marry and no intention to wait to consummate it. Crabtree stops them, arrests the poor boy and chastises Penny. However, Crabtree is a romantic, and he can see how in love the two young people are. He insists they be chaperoned until they are married, but Crabtree is never one to stand in the way of true love.

Of all the regular characters in *Murdoch Mysteries*, Crabtree, it may be argued, has grown the most over the eight seasons. He began as a simple man with simple desires in life, but as the years have passed his natural curiosity and capacity to learn quickly have made him more ambitious. Having always wanted a family, Crabtree now wants advancement in his career as well. He has even tried his hand at creative pursuits, publishing a rollicking tale of Egyptian curses and adventure. A relative success, Crabtree continues to burn with creative ideas, though he can never seem to quite decide what his now much-anticipated second novel will be.

Straightforward and charming, Crabtree is utterly guileless. A good man with a steady job, the constable is a good prospect for the average working woman in Toronto. Yet his simple, self-effacing honesty attracts women far above his own social standing as well. His one true love is the subject of much fan and show-writer debate, but it can be said that he has at least met his match in Dr Emily Grace.

### Playing opposite Jonny's Crabtree has been one of the greatest joys in my life. Yannick Bisson, *Detective William Murdoch*

Crabtree may not have much in the way of schooling, but his life has been an education. He is thoughtful and sometimes philosophical. He may not understand Murdoch's scientific ramblings, but he does understand people. A natural optimist, he is always prepared to give the benefit of the doubt. Where Brackenreid may believe that humanity is more inclined to evil than good, Crabtree always sees the potential for good and the possibility for redemption. Through Crabtree we have hope that the world he perceives may one day come to be.

Constable Higgins (Lachlan Murdoch) and acting Detective Crabtree walk the crime scene (209).

## MOTHER

**IN SEASON 2, CRABTREE FEELS** he must search for his birth mother. He places an advert in the classifieds and innocently trusts that whomever answers it will be his mother. Of course he doesn't imagine that his steady salary and pension could attract a pretender to the title. To settle the issue, Murdoch arranges for Crabtree to be shot – in a bullet-proof vest, of course – and has Ogden verify the severity of his "injuries" to his would-be mothers. Murdoch's plan works. Only a real mother would be willing to care for a disabled son she had just met, and so Crabtree finds his birth mother at last.

### Did You Know?

When Crabtree was searching for his mother in season 2, the two women who answer his ad are named Emily and Gracie. But before we take that as a sign that Crabtree is destined to be with Emily Grace, it's worth noting that the woman who actually is his mother, Gracie, has the last name of Brooks, as in Edna Brooks. Coincidence?

# FLOWER AUNTS

**Amaryllis, Aster, Azalea, Begonia, Begonia II, Bryony, Clematis, Dahlia, Daisy, Hyacinth, Iris, Ivy, Petunia, Primrose, Magnolia, Marigold, Nettle, Rose. . .**

**THROUGHOUT THE MANY SEASONS,** Crabtree references various aunts in anecdotes that may (or may not) be appropriate to the situation at hand. These aunts are seemingly innumerable, and their relevance to situations inexhaustible. Though tiresome to Murdoch and Brackenreid, the recurring theme of Crabtree's aunts is a source of constant amusement to the audience. We wait to hear about yet the next aunt, and the next.

For many seasons the aunts remained a mystery. Just how did Crabtree, a foundling, manage to accrue so many? How big was the family of the Reverend who adopted him? And why were they all named after flowers?

I think it's brilliant how the writers brought the innumerable aunts gag to a reality. They had to work around certain facts that had already been established:

1. He was a foundling.
2. He has a Newfoundland accent.
3. He has referenced a zillion florally monikered aunts.

So, in season 7, during an investigation that leads Crabtree and Murdoch to St. John's, we get the whole story. George was partly raised by a minister and his family in Toronto and then brought to Newfoundland. That minister helped a group of prostitutes who faced the perils of violent street life by renting them a rectory, under two conditions: They were to run a "respectable" business – all clients had to wear a tie – and they had to attend church services on Sunday.

Crabtree was raised and nurtured by a bunch of really nice prostitutes. Maybe that's why he's a little weird.

– *Jonny Harris, Constable George Crabtree*

### Did You Know?

Aunt Begonia has been mentioned twice in the series. First in episode 311 'The Curse of Beaton Manor' as having died laughing. Then again in episode 611 'Twisted Sisters', seemingly having risen from the dead and tailored Crabtree a suit. In truth, upon the first Aunt Begonia's passing, a flower name was then made available, and one of Crabtree's newer "aunts" quickly snapped it up. Aunt Begonia II!

## CASTING GEORGE CRABTREE

Cal Coons was looking to create a character for the TV series, to be called Crabtree, who would continue to fill the same role as his namesake from the Murdoch books, as Murdoch's sidekick. A character who could do all of the regular, unglamorous police work and fill in information gaps where needed. Every great detective has an invaluable sidekick, and Crabtree was to be to Murdoch what Watson is to Sherlock. He also wanted to use the character to introduce some humour into the show, helping shift the tone towards the lighter side.

When Cal went to cast this important character, he was hoping to find someone who would be inherently funny, but not in a buffoonish way. He also needed to find an actor who could convey intelligence despite a lack of a formal education, and have an innocence and naivete.

The Crabtree in the books is a big, burly, oafish man. Jonny Harris is the exact opposite of that, but when he walked into the audition room, there was something about his warmth that attracted Cal instantly. He read the role with an understated humour, a bit off key, and his Newfoundlander accent only added to the charm. In the Victorian era, Toronto residents were mainly from the British Isles, and there was a broad mash-up of accents and slang amongst the working classes. Jonny's natural accent felt right at home with that historical context, even though Cal hadn't been on the lookout for an accent at all.

"When I first got the audition and read the breakdown of the character Crabtree, it implied that he was a large, intimidating figure, the muscle of the group," Jonny remembers. "I was shocked when I found out I got a callback. When I went in and met Christina Jennings and Cal Coons they explained they were going in a different direction with Crabtree. He was going to be a bit of a quirky thinker, he was going to bring some levity to the show. I thought, 'Okay, that's more like it. I have a chance at this.'"

Cal has said that, when casting, an actor needs to somehow stand out, be something more or better than what the producer is expecting. Jonny was completely off their radar when he came in to read, but his warmth, modesty and the sort of small-town innocence he exuded were not only a good fit for the character, but for the Victorian era as well.

Murdoch and the constabulary come face to face with a werewolf (212).

Above: Grace fights back against a zombie (705).

Right: The ghost of Queen's Park (607).

# The World According to
## GEORGE CRABTREE

Crabtree is fun to watch, fun for Jonny to play, and fun for the writers to write. He can go off on any sort of wild theory, at any time, and in any context. His way of seeing the world is unique and refreshing.

## SUPERNATURAL TRUTHS

Martians, werewolves, voodoo, goblins, vampires, sasquatches (but *not* abominable snowmen), leprechauns, Venusians, ghosts, revenants, sea monsters (but *not* lake monsters)… Crabtree never hesitates to try and solve a mystery with a supernatural explanation. He has run the gamut from ancient curses to zombies. No matter how many times he is proven wrong, he refuses to accept that these phenomena may not actually exist.

An avid reader, Crabtree's child-like glee at the potential for these otherworldly creatures to actually exist imbues episodes such as 'Werewolves', 'Bloodlust' and 'Evil Eye of Egypt' with a certain wonder, a certain innocence, and a certain delight. We can all remember a time when we too believed in ghosts. Watching as Crabtree attempts to prove his theories, we can't help but support his endeavours.

And Crabtree is almost never entirely wrong. There really was a werewolf, even if it was strictly speaking a man in a wolf's skin. There really were zombies, even if they were manipulated by brain surgery. There really was a vampire, albeit a haemophiliac who required blood transfusions to stay alive. Without Crabtree's tendency to hypothesise about the impossible, Murdoch just might not uncover the implausible truth.

*Dr Luther Bates (Mike Shara) is killed by his own creation (705).*

*Crabtree is a thinker, let's give him that. He's got a great imagination that can, at times, misfire most brilliantly.*

Jonny Harris, *Constable George Crabtree*

## MAN OF THE FUTURE

Crabtree may not be much of a scientist, but he is on the cutting edge of innovations in other areas. He can smell a good idea, and has proved that he has a real nose for business. Destined to be a millionaire in the future, Crabtree has invested in some start-up companies that we know will be hugely successful corporations within his lifetime, Ford Motors, Standard Oil, Coca-Cola, IBM, Bell Telephone and General Electric among them. But where Crabtree is truly ahead of the times is with food. He tries to convince a skeptical Murdoch that coffee is the next big thing. Then pizza, perhaps even delivered to your door, seems like a sure-fire hit. Grace wins him over to the side of the hot hamburger, an early version of the mainstay it is today.

Crabtree can see what Murdoch cannot, the practical, everyday application of almost all of Murdoch's inventions, whereas Murdoch can only see one purpose, the one for which it was built. Murdoch can't quite open his mind enough to appreciate the practicality of a potato-cooking room (our modern microwave), or a board game which requires the players to solve a murder (Clue). Some of Crabtree's ideas may not be fully realized, like a horse that runs backwards, but his creative mind never ceases to find innovative ways of improving life. Some of his more notable thoughts include tweeting, mobile phones, paint by numbers, and the infamous Constable Crabtree's Household Adhesive Strips (quickly renamed Murdoch and Crabtree's Household Adhesive Strips). Crabtree is a man of the future, only his future is that of the everyman. And we thank him for it.

## WRITTEN BY GEORGE CRABTREE

While Crabtree may not think to patent every idea that flits through his hyperactive brain, he does occasionally write them down. Much like Watson did with Sherlock, Crabtree realizes that his job provides him with a wealth of material for a fantastical adventure novel. His penchant for all things supernatural leads him to an Egyptian curse, and he sees himself in the dashing detective who saves the day. The novel finished, Crabtree never ceases to inform everyone of his next project, though we've yet to see a finished copy. But his never-ending research into these unfinished masterpieces tends to come in handy in the course of Murdoch's investigations. At the very least, Crabtree's writings, or lack thereof, have educated him on a vast array of topics. He may not have gone to school, but he has certainly become a man of the world. Even if that world is all in his head.

*Crabtree proudly displaying his first novel,* The Curse of the Pharaohs *(503).*

*Murdoch and Crabtree discover the shooting mechanism (509).*

*Crabtree and Grace watch the fireworks at midnight (513).*

*Emily Grace and Crabtree (504).*

*Crabtree and Grace enjoy a day at the ____ (7).*

# The Loves of
# GEORGE CRABTREE

Crabtree's life revolves around his work, but he still finds time to enjoy the pleasures of the city, usually with Constable Henry Higgins by his side. But there are times when Crabtree finds himself in the company of a young lady, and over the years there have been a few.

## RUBY OGDEN

Though Ruby first laid her beguiling eye on Murdoch solely to ruffle her sister's feathers, when she and Crabtree are thrown together on a case, she can't help but find he is much more than a thick-headed constable. Ruby is won over by Crabtree's thoughtfulness and compassion, and Crabtree finds himself entranced with her beauty and irrepressible spirit. However, they are from different worlds, and Ruby is not a girl to be pinned down. Some fans hope for a Ruby and George reunion, but her worldliness may be what will keep these two apart.

## EMILY GRACE

When Grace arrives in season 5, Crabtree isn't sure what to make of her. Her irreverent attitude at the scene of the crime is at once off-putting and intriguing. Then she takes him seriously in his role of acting detective, and he is, in that moment, won over.

The two find themselves like peas in a pod. Equally enthusiastic at work – though admittedly their enthusiasm could not be engendered by more different subjects – they find a kindred spirit in one another and can't help but seek each other out. Grace's curiosity rivals that of Crabtree's, and he quickly learns that she is up for any kind of adventure, be it culinary or otherworldly. Their romance blooms, and they enjoy one another's company immensely. Nevertheless, Grace is a professional woman, with a university education and Crabtree can't help but feel some inferiority to her, though Grace never notices. When Leslie Garland enters the picture, Crabtree is consumed by jealousy. An innocent flirtation causes him tremendous worry, and in a moment of jealous rage he ends their relationship. Hotly contested amongst fans as to who was actually at fault for their breakup, both share at least some of the blame. Crabtree for allowing his doubts to overpower him and Grace for allowing herself to be tempted by another man. But they will always care for one another. Fans pulling for "Gemily" (George plus Emily) will simply have to wait and see.

## EDNA BROOKS NEE GARRISON ✱✱✱✱✱✱✱✱✱✱✱✱✱✱✱✱✱✱✱✱✱✱✱✱✱✱✱✱✱✱✱✱✱✱✱

In the very first episode of the series we are introduced to Crabtree as both constable and wooer of women when he is adorably awkward with Edna Garrison, an animal rights activist and, at that time, suspect in a murder. He finds himself attracted to her spirit, and manages to win a date with her, by pretending to woo her dog. We see nothing of Edna after this episode and imagine their flirtation to have been nothing more than that. Until season 8, when Edna suddenly reappears, as a war widow and stepmother to an unruly son. Her reappearance comes at a perfect time for Crabtree, months after his split with Grace. Crabtree rekindles his relationship with Edna, though the years have dampened her spirit somewhat, and the two fall quickly into a comfortable routine. Crabtree has an instant family, and feels secure in the life ahead when he proposes and she accepts. Then it all falls apart, quickly and brutally, leaving Crabtree alone and in trouble. Fans of "Gedna" (George plus Edna) were upset at the shocking change in fortune after investing so much in their courtship. Crabtree and Edna share a comfortable love, but arguably not a great passion, and the trial before them may be too much for their fledgling romance to bear.

*Animal rights protester Edna Garrison (Tamara Hope) has words with Crabtree (101).*

*Edna Brooks (Tamara Hope) congratulates Crabtree on his wrestling victory (816).*

*Above: Crabtree and Edna Brooks celebrate their engagement with a kiss and Crabtree gives Edna the good news about his promotion to detective. (817).*

*Crabtree reflects on his promotion at his desk (816).*

*Detective Hamish Slorach (Patrick McKenna), Crabtree and Brackenreid try to piece together evidence to find Murdoch (301).*

*Desk Sergeant Armstrong (Prime Minister Stephen Harper) and Crabtree (407).*

*Crabtree sifts through files (511).*

## SETTING GEORGE CRABTREE ✿✿✿✿✿✿✿✿✿✿✿✿✿✿✿✿✿✿✿✿✿✿✿✿✿✿✿✿✿✿✿✿✿✿✿✿✿✿✿✿✿✿✿✿✿✿✿✿✿✿

Crabtree's desk stands in the space between Murdoch and Brackenreid's offices, meaning he is in full view, and shouting distance, of both his superiors. Often working on a task for one or the other, Crabtree is therefore in the perfect position to present his findings or be called into action.

His desk is standard and matches that of the many other constables' desks throughout the bullpen, including being furnished with a typewriter. Not all of the typewriters in the bullpen are still functioning, as they are all relatively authentic to the period, but Craig Grant makes sure that the one on Crabtree's desk always works.

There is always a copy of *Curse of the Pharaohs* in Crabtree's desk drawer, just in case anyone should have misplaced theirs. Because Crabtree has such a small space, there is no other specific set dressing to help enhance his character, though his helmet is a constant companion on the corner of his desk. Often times it will also be scattered with files or mug shots of the case he is working on that day. The set dressers are mindful of what Crabtree is doing at any given time, and always make sure that his desk is ready to help him find the right information so that Murdoch can solve the case.

## DRESSING GEORGE CRABTREE ❖❖❖❖❖❖❖❖❖❖❖❖❖❖❖❖❖❖❖❖❖❖❖❖❖❖❖❖❖❖❖❖❖❖❖❖

Alex Reda was able to find actual photographs of the constables at the real Police Station No. 4 in the 1890s, so he had the ideal reference point for their uniforms. He and his team tried to replicate the uniforms as closely as possible, right down to the "4" badges on the collar. The helmets had to be specially cast to match the helmets of the time, and the maple-leaf badge on the front of them is a perfect match to what a constable on the streets of Toronto would have worn. Alex was also thrilled when he was able to find original leather belts with the snake buckle detail, exactly as worn by the police.

*The blue uniform isn't a bad look, I think it's quite sharp.*

Jonny Harris, *Constable George Crabtree*

As the seasons progress, we see Crabtree more and more in civilian clothing. The key was to make sure his suit was different from that of Murdoch or Brackenreid, and be fitting of his working class station in life, and of a quality that makes sense on a constable's salary. Alex also chose a bowler hat for Crabtree, as it was the most popular hat with the average man of Victorian Toronto.

*Crabtree has bet on Murdoch to win the cycling race (702).*

*Crabtree arrives in Haileybury on his trusty donkey steed (811).*

**Did You Know?**

Jonny Harris always keeps his cell phone in a pocket of his constable uniform, and he doesn't always remember to turn the ringer off. It's very confusing while acting in a scene involving early twentieth-century technology, when his twenty-first-century technology interrupts!

*Crabtree questions the pizza man (Tony DeSantis) and tries a bite (603).*

# *Inspector*
# THOMAS BRACKENREID

"*If it turns out to be a Martian that did this,*
*I want him handcuffed, booked,*
*and sitting in my cell.*"

# Inspector THOMAS BRACKENREID

Every great police detective has a demanding and ornery boss. In Murdoch's case, that role falls to Inspector Thomas Brackenreid. Cal Coons was looking to include a character who would be in charge of Murdoch and, while he would always be Murdoch's ally, he would not always see the world, or the crime, in the same way.

*Brackenreid faces pressure from his backers in his run for Alderman to score political points by evicting a band of gypsies (409).*

Brackenreid is a tough army man from Yorkshire, England. The eldest of five boys, he left school at a young age to help feed his hungry brothers. He served with Her Majesty's army in Afghanistan, as he is fond of mentioning at every opportunity. Upon his return to England he decided he would try his luck in the colonies, where he met his wife, Margaret Brackenreid, and settled into a decent life as a constable at Station No. 4. He rose through the ranks with relative ease, returning to Station No. 4 as its inspector, and was given Detective William Murdoch as his right-hand man.

*Brackenreid and a group of Aldermen (502).*

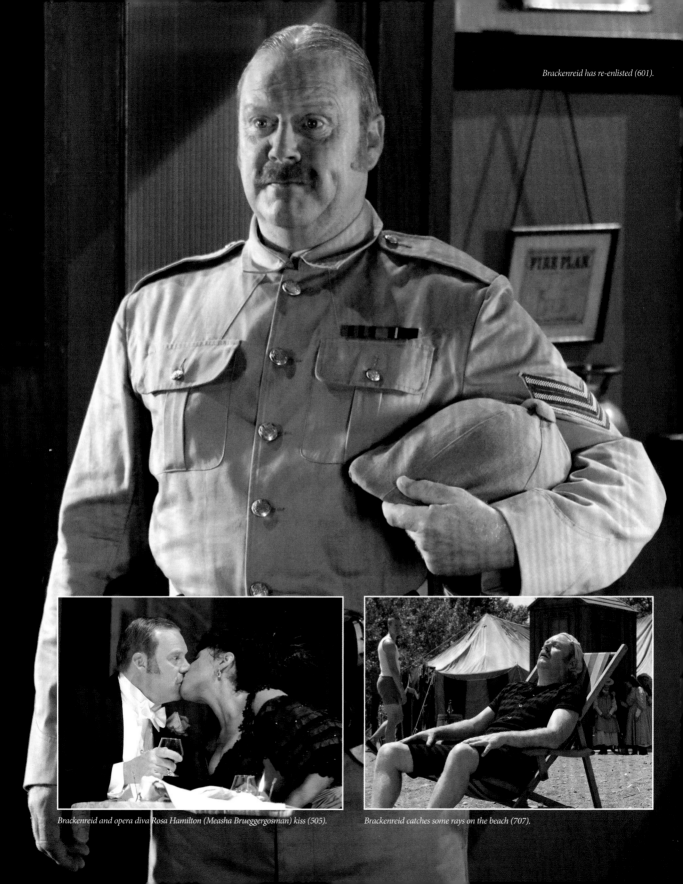

Brackenreid has re-enlisted (601).

Brackenreid and opera diva Rosa Hamilton (Measha Brueggergosman) kiss (505).

Brackenreid catches some rays on the beach (707).

He could not come from a more different background than Murdoch, and initially could not be more in opposition to Murdoch's way of approaching his cases. Where Murdoch is ingeniously cerebral, Brackenreid is brutally physical. He comes from the old school of policing. Men succumb to force, and criminals deserve no better.

Over the years, Brackenreid gradually learns to appreciate Murdoch's less confrontational style. He even tries it out for himself, with varying degrees of success. But Brackenreid is who he is, and plays to his strengths.

Brackenreid isn't all fists and intimidation, though. He has a softer side, and a surprising affinity for the arts. A lover of Shakespeare and the opera, Brackenreid elevates himself above his middle-class position, a self-educated man in the finer things of Victorian life. His love for his family also supersedes his rough and tumble persona, and we see him as a loving and attentive father, if not a bit traditional in his hopes for his children.

A Victorian man, Brackenreid represents the views and understanding of the average man of the times. Through Brackenreid, the audience can see some of the historical context for Murdoch's more advanced theories or Ogden's modern viewpoints on social issues. Brackenreid is our window into the Victorian soul. As such, even he can't help but change as the years go by, broadening his perspectives and loosening his rigid understanding of the world. At his heart he remains a man of the times in which he lives. And we wouldn't want him any other way.

## BRACKENREID AT WORK

Inspector Brackenreid runs a tight ship. He is fair but demanding, and the constables of Station No. 4 know better than to shirk their duties or clock in late for their shifts. Always one to lead by example, Brackenreid is the consummate professional. He even goes so far as to arrest his own wife when she involves herself in an illegal lottery scheme. His one vice is a teacup filled with whiskey just as often as it is with tea, but even this is perfectly acceptable behaviour for a Victorian man hard at work. Besides, his slightly addictive personality makes liquor the better choice, as his experiments with medicinal cocaine and heroin demonstrate all too well.

His men are fiercely loyal to him and to each other, and that includes Detective Murdoch and Constable Crabtree. In a way Brackenreid is the great father figure of the series. He cares deeply for those he is closest to, and tries in his own way to help each of them succeed in life. A family man at heart, and a leader in the truest sense, Station No. 4 is as much his family as Margaret and his two sons, and he will do anything for his men. This loyalty is what bonds him to Murdoch, and Murdoch to him.

With nothing in common outside of work, Brackenreid and Murdoch are not really friends as such, but share a bond closer to that of family. They have their differences, but they have also gained a deep respect for one another over the years. Their bond solidifies when Brackenreid covers for Murdoch's only major transgression, at the end of season 4, when Murdoch allows a confessed murderess to escape Station No. 4's cells. This lie by omission by Brackenreid to his superiors, not undertaken lightly by him, now runs underneath his and Murdoch's relationship. Neither had done such a thing before, and neither has since, but a transgression of such magnitude, in direct opposition to the badge each wears so proudly, is a silent pact between two honourable men.

Brackenreid takes Murdoch's well-being to heart, and spends an inordinate amount of time subtly attempting to help him win Ogden's hand, or keep her hand from falling into someone else's. He also feels the need to give Murdoch unwanted relationship advice from time to time, which always makes Murdoch enormously uncomfortable. He only wants Murdoch to solve the case and win the girl, wishes that are ultimately granted.

Brackenreid is also fatherly with Crabtree, but in a slightly more irritated way. Crabtree is a good copper, and he does his job with unwavering enthusiasm. Brackenreid appreciates that, but along with Crabtree's enthusiasm comes a stream of outlandish theories about the case at hand. Brackenreid is not one to go off on a flight of fancy, so when Crabtree starts to rattle off his latest crazy idea, Brackenreid tends to lose patience quickly. Then the one time Brackenreid is ready to accept an outlandish explanation for a murder, in the form of a lake monster, Crabtree is the theory's only opposition! Doomed to disagree for eternity, Crabtree nonetheless occupies a place in Brackenreid's heart, and much like with Murdoch, Brackenreid would do anything for him in the end.

### Brackenreid thinks of Crabtree as an errant nephew.

Thomas Craig, *Inspector Thomas Brackenreid*

Of course Brackenreid can't help but be protective of the women of the series, too. Not only his wife, but Ogden and Grace as well. He can foresee the consequences of the decisions the two doctors make, and takes it upon himself to educate them as such. It is not always received well, as is the case when Ogden considers running for provincial government office, or when he warns Grace that her dalliance with Lillian Moss may have serious consequences. While his manner may not be the most gentle, however, his intentions are always pure. Crusty on the outside and soft in the middle, Thomas Brackenreid only wants what is best for everyone, and will do what he feels he must to ensure it.

*Margaret Brackrenreid (Arwen Humphreys) and her husband (716).*

# MARGARET BRACKENREID

A GRUFF MAN LIKE BRACKENREID needs a spitfire of a wife. No shrinking violet, Margaret Brackenreid is the ideal counterpart to her classic Victorian husband. Equally a product of the times, Margaret may not buy into votes for women, but she has learned from the women who went before her how to manage a husband without him knowing. An ardent member of the Temperance League, Margaret's main struggle in life is keeping her husband off the sauce, with little to no success. Though she's not a paragon of virtue herself. Involvement in an illegal lottery scheme puts her on the wrong side of the law, and her jealous streak has put at least one opera singer on the wrong end of her umbrella. But she is a good mother and a loyal wife, the classic great woman behind her great man.

## Did You Know?

There was some discussion early on as to whether Thomas Craig's real-life family might play his onscreen family. They were visiting in Canada while Mrs Brackenreid's scenes in season 1 were being filmed. But what would happen if they went to season 2? His wife and kids couldn't just pick up from England every time Mrs B was needed, so the search and Arwen Humphreys was cast in...

## THE BRACKENREIDS ✰✰✰✰✰✰✰✰✰✰✰✰✰✰✰✰✰✰✰✰✰✰✰✰✰✰✰✰✰✰✰✰✰✰✰✰✰✰

Brackenreid is very much a family man. His marriage to Margaret is the model for successful relationships throughout the series. They have their differences, alcohol being the most troublesome, but their genuine love and affection for one another is evident regardless of the tone of their conversation. Thomas Craig always enjoys it when his onscreen wife makes an appearance in an episode. Her presence gives Brackenreid another dimension, and forces him out of his leadership role into a slightly less confident position. When this happens in the station house, it's always a source of delight for both the constables and the audience at home.

*The Brackenreids have the hottest relationship on the show.*
*The ginseng scene [in 'Kung Fu Crabtree'] was super hot.*
Arwen Humphreys, *Margaret Brackenreid*

His two sons, John and Bobby, have their place in the series as well. When Bobby goes missing in a case of mistaken identity in season 3, we see just how tightly knit the Brackenreid family is. Brackenreid may work long hours and have grave things on his mind, but he is always attentive with his boys. He wants a better life for them than he had growing up, and he is fiercely protective of them. No matter what, Brackenreid's family always comes first.

Brackenreid hugs his son Bobby (Gage Munroe), who had been kidnapped (304).

Brackenreid goes fishing with his sons John (Charles Vandervaart) and Bobby (Jayden

## CASTING THOMAS BRACKENREID

A British actor seemed like the appropriate approach for Brackenreid, and the search was on to find the right man for the job. Thomas Craig remembers being asked by his agent to send a reel to Shaftesbury in Canada, as she had run out of them. He didn't think anything of it, nor did he know what the show was, until he received a call asking him to tape an audition. Cal Coons instantly liked what he saw. Not only did Thomas have a good look for the part, with his ginger hair and authentic face, but he aced the reading. He had the right amount of gruff, without making the character a cartoon. Also key to Brackenreid was a sense of humour, which Thomas managed to portray even on his short audition tapes. Thomas was offered the role and accepted it, still not really knowing anything about what he had signed on to, and never expecting the show would last so many years. For his part, Cal was excited Thomas accepted the role, as an actor of his caliber would be a huge asset to the show. Once again, Cal's instinct was dead right.

## SETTING THOMAS BRACKENREID

Brackenreid's office is the one space dedicated to his character. It has a place of prominence in Station No. 4, befitting his rank and stature. He has a private entrance directly leading to the front door, which can allow his character to move about or entertain prominent guests with some delicacy, if necessary.

When Sandy Kybartas and Armando Sgrignuoli were approaching the set design in Brackenreid's office, they wanted to keep it simple. Not too much should be revealed by his surroundings to those who visit him, and an air of authority needed to be present.

The dark furnishings are in keeping with his traditional values and enhance the gravity of a visit to the inspector's office. A portrait of the reigning monarch on the wall befits his English upbringing. Brackenreid reminds us that Canada was but a small part of the vast British Empire of the late nineteenth century, and his office reflects that old-world power.

Armando also made sure to leave room for Brackenreid's office to grow along with his character. Since the baseball

*Below: Brackenreid during the baseball game (508).*

*Brackenreid shares war stories with Arthur (Rick Hughes) and Harry Hendrickson (Jamie Abrams) in his office (601).*

*Brackenreid reads a threatening letter addressed to him (102).*

*Right: Yannick Bisson and Thomas Craig on a break between scenes, on the S.S. Keewatin (701).*

*Opposite: An Alex Reda costume design for one of Brackenreid's work suits.*

*Did You Know?*

Thomas Craig is the only one of the main cast who always wears period-accurate footwear on set, whether his shoes will be seen on camera or not.

tournament in season 5, a team photo of the Station No. 4 constables in their baseball uniforms proudly occupies a prime spot behind Brackenreid's chair. With his recent forays into artistic expression in evidence through his latest avant-garde paintings.

## DRESSING THOMAS BRACKENREID

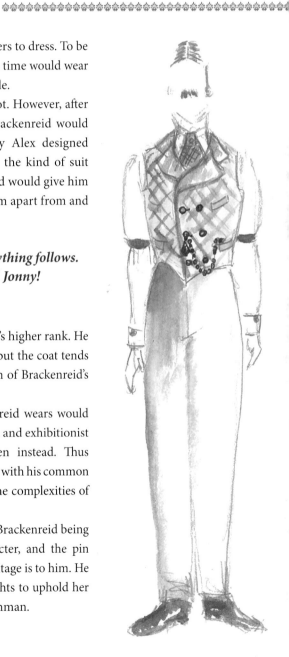

Alex Reda found Brackenreid one of the trickier characters to dress. To be historically accurate, a police inspector in Toronto at the time would wear a distinct uniform, fancier than that of a regular constable.

So Alex created a replica of this uniform for the pilot. However, after it was shot, Cal Coons and Christina Jennings felt Brackenreid would benefit from wearing civilian clothing. Consequently Alex designed a suit for him that would work as a sort of uniform, the kind of suit Brackenreid would wear specifically as an inspector, and would give him the authority his character commands, while setting him apart from and above Murdoch.

*My approach to Brackenreid was to get the hair right and everything follows. Also, always wear the correct footwear – take note Yannick and Jonny!*

Thomas Craig, *Inspector Thomas Brackenreid*

Alex chose a frock suit as emblematic of Brackenreid's higher rank. He has a variety of waistcoats for Brackenreid to alternate, but the coat tends to remain the same. Alex chose to do this as a reflection of Brackenreid's traditional character.

The proper hat to go with the type of suit Brackenreid wears would actually be a top hat, but Alex felt that would be too posh and exhibitionist for Brackenreid, so a simple bowler hat was chosen instead. Thus Brackenreid's daily "uniform" combines his elevated rank with his common beginnings, making his clothing an ideal reflection of the complexities of his character.

As a final touch, Alex added a St George's cross pin. Brackenreid being an Englishman is a very important part of his character, and the pin reminds us of that and how important Brackenreid's heritage is to him. He fought for Mother England in the army, and now he fights to uphold her laws in her colonies. He is, and always will be, an Englishman.

# Doctor
# EMILY GRACE

*"Your gut...*
*is that similar to women's intuition?"*

# Doctor EMILY GRACE

Season 5 of *Murdoch Mysteries* brought about great changes on the show. Murdoch had compromised his principles by letting a murderess go free, and had implicated Brackenreid in the cover up. Ogden had married Darcy Garland, despite making her true feelings known to Murdoch. Murdoch was broken hearted, and had found himself in the Yukon, about as far away from Ogden as possible. The relationships had shifted, and with them, the dynamic of the show. The producers and networks were interested in introducing a second female lead character. The search was on to find a dynamic new character to enhance the already well-established world of *Murdoch Mysteries*.

*Murdoch and Grace with the Egyptian mummy (503).*

*Dr Grace surveys Diane's (Brittany Johnson) body, found in the woods (714).*

Enter Dr Emily Grace. Introduced as Ogden's protégée, Grace quickly impresses Crabtree with her wit and enthusiasm for the job at hand. Energetic and improper, Grace has little time for politeness. The thrill of discovery trumps any social graces and her blunt honesty both irritates and amuses. A breath of fresh air, Grace and Crabtree find common ground in their unconventionally adventurous spirits. Competent and helpful, Grace initially annoys Murdoch to no end, but she quickly proves herself more than capable to do the job. Murdoch will just need some time to accept anyone other than Ogden in the morgue.

A woman of some mystery, we only have the barest of hints about Grace's past. We know she was once engaged to Jerome Bradley, an upper-class hockey player who claims to have brought her up into society. We know she excels at croquet, but was only able to join the Toronto Athletic Club because of that same engagement. We also know she dabbles in death experiments, hoping to see a glimpse of the afterlife. Hints at a middle-class past make us curious as to how exactly Grace became a doctor. Though a few years behind Ogden, women were still uncommon in the professional schools. Often only those with connections and money could manage their way through the opposition. Despite not having grown up as Ogden's equal, evident in her brusque manner, Grace certainly has the intellect and talent to excel in her chosen field. Ogden would not have groomed her to take over otherwise.

*What's going to pee on me today?*

Georgina Reilly, *Dr Emily Grace*

Grace's fixation with death and what lies beyond grounds her character in the macabre. Less compassionate towards the bodies on the slab than her predecessor, Grace revels in the mystery of what the body has to say. And she will do whatever is necessary to find the truth.

Definitely not squeamish, Grace has no qualms in using animals in her multiple experiments. She has gleefully performed post-mortems on snakes, gerbils, numerous rats and even spiders. Georgina Reilly remembers one of her first days on set involved cutting open a pickled snake. The smell is what she remembers the most – formaldehyde and death. But she girded herself to the task, and despite a moment of hesitation, she channeled the spirit of the unflappable Emily Grace and just did it. Georgina has since become accustomed to the creatures in Grace's morgue. Not squeamish herself, she just likes to be prepared for whatever experiment Grace is throwing at her. Georgina will now walk on set expecting to have to deal with laboratory animals – and their accompanying by-products.

## THE LOVES OF EMILY GRACE

Romantically, Grace has made some controversial choices, with one exception. Her effervescent introduction in season 5 piques the interest of Crabtree, and the two slowly find common ground and a certain delight in one another's unconventional thinking. An attraction grows, and Grace and Crabtree find themselves searching for moments to share, both investigatively and personally. When Toronto is threatened by a mad bomber and the city is being evacuated, Crabtree takes his opportunity and kisses Grace for the first time. It was a kiss she would not soon forget, and their relationship begins in earnest.

However, despite their obvious attraction to one another, Crabtree and Grace always kept their relationship casual. There was never any talk of marriage or children. They simply enjoyed one another's company. So when Leslie Garland, the younger brother of Ogden's deceased husband, Darcy Garland, emerges handsomely from the glittering waters of Lake Ontario, Grace can't help but take notice.

Her head may have been turned by Leslie's good looks and charm, but Grace never considers anything beyond an innocent flirtation. She may be impulsive, but she is not unfaithful. Only when forced to kiss Leslie while undercover to avoid being outed does Grace succumb to her attraction. When Crabtree's subsequent jealous attack on her causes them to end their relationship, Grace turns to Leslie for comfort.

*Leslie Garland (Giacomo Gianniotti) runs into Grace at the Blind Pig club (710).*

*Lillian Moss (Sara Mitich) shares a tender moment with Grace (814).*

*Grace and Crabtree react to shopkeeper Milne calling her a trollop (504).*

### Did You Know?

When Giacomo Gianniotti (Leslie Garland) and Georgina were filming their scene in the ragtime bar in 'Murdoch in Ragtime', director Harvey Crossland had them yell their lines at one another as though there was loud music in the background. The music was added in later, but at the time both of them felt rather foolish since they were yelling at each other over perfect silence!

*Grace and Lillian Moss (Sara Mitich) are brought to a back room at the nightclub (814).*

*Grace and Ogden are eager to hear adventurer Elva Gordon's lecture (711).*

Just as Grace chose badly with Jerome Bradley, so too does she fail to see behind Leslie's pretty facade. Used as a pawn in his game of revenge against Ogden and Murdoch, Grace is left betrayed and embarrassed. Any potential reunion with Crabtree seems impossible, and Grace finds she could use a respite from the tumult of her love life.

Grace throws herself into her work, finding a cause that inspires her and inflames her passion more than any man – that of women's suffrage. Through this Grace meets Lillian Moss. Lillian woos Grace, perhaps not quite with Grace's conscious knowledge. But Grace finds herself reciprocating Lillian's advances, much to her own surprise.

Brackenreid warns her what an open relationship with another woman could mean to Grace's hard-fought career, no matter how hard she tries to keep it hidden. Relations between women may not be illegal, but they are certainly not acceptable. However, Grace sees Lillian as more than just a woman. Lillian is dangerous, exciting, and a crusader. Lillian brings out a side of Grace she never knew existed. She helps Grace become more than just her work. A dangerous liaison at a time when society did not accept alternative relationships, their affair may change Grace's life in ways she cannot foresee.

## CASTING EMILY GRACE ✿✿✿✿✿✿✿✿✿✿✿✿✿✿✿✿✿✿✿✿✿✿✿✿✿✿✿✿✿✿✿✿✿✿✿✿✿✿✿✿✿✿✿✿✿

The net was cast quite widely for the actor who would play the new coroner. She would need to stand apart from Ogden, carry herself differently and approach the new role in a fresh way. Georgina Reilly had auditioned for *Murdoch Mysteries* before, for a role in season 3. At the time she was disappointed not to be cast, but in hindsight she's thankful – had she already been on the show she would not have been in the running for the new and integral part of Dr Emily Grace.

She came well prepared, ready to recite an interminably long speech of medical jargon, dressed in Victorian-style clothing and with her hair up. Peter Mitchell, showrunner from season 5 onwards, was on the lookout for someone as prepared as she was talented. On a show like *Murdoch Mysteries*, with a tight shooting schedule, and for a character like Dr Grace whose speeches are often long and complicated, an actor who could handle the language and the pressure would be key. Georgina instantly impressed on both accounts.

However, Georgina remembers not feeling particularly positive after her first audition, so when she was called back to read with Yannick, she was thrilled. But she remembers being confused. She knew that the coroner was Yannick's love interest. She hadn't been told what the plans were for the character of Dr Grace, or Murdoch and Ogden, so she wasn't quite sure what to do in her next audition. Should she be flirtatious

*Murdoch and Grace prepare to take the dead man's fingermarks (511).*

**Did You Know?**

The shelving in the morgue on the experiment table once sat in the laboratory of Frederick Banting and Charles Best (Nobel-Prize winners who discovered insulin in 1921). An authentic piece of medical innovation that reflects the fictional innovation which it continues to witness on *Murdoch Mysteries*!

or not? Her question was never answered, and whatever she did in the callback worked. She remembers how supportive Yannick was, and how confident she felt by the end. She was right, of course, to feel that way, as she won the role and has since made Dr Grace her own.

Her first day was a bit of a blur. Production had already started on season 5 and the crew was in full swing. Yannick was also directing that episode, 'Murdoch at the Opera', which only added to her already significant nerves. The first scene Georgina shot was with Thomas Craig, as Grace reports to Brackenreid. Dr Grace enters the police station, spouts off an enormous chunk of medical dialogue, and leaves. She recalls Thomas being supportive and kind, reassuring her that she was doing a good job. It was intimidating, but she pulled it off and has been mastering the jargon ever since. She quickly won over the rest of the cast and crew with her positivity and enthusiasm – much like Emily Grace quickly won over Murdoch and his colleagues – and there are now legions of fans devoted to the fate of her character.

## SETTING EMILY GRACE ✦✦✦✦✦✦✦✦✦✦✦✦✦✦✦✦✦✦✦✦✦✦✦✦✦✦✦✦✦✦✦✦✦✦✦✦✦✦✦✦✦✦✦✦

As the set design strives to provide comfortable and authentic places for the characters who inhabit them, so the morgue needed to change to accommodate its new mistress, Dr Emily Grace. The differences are subtle, but upon closer inspection they are there. Gone are the goldfish and phonograph of Ogden's time. In their place are now terrariums with plants and animals, not so much to enliven the environment like Ogden's goldfish, but to signify Grace's unquenchable curiosity about the world around her. As she experiments on animals, so too might she experiment with plants, observing their life cycles and reactions to stimuli. Not one to linger over beauty for its own sake, Grace surrounds herself with experiments and their results.

Georgina loves the morgue. The set is beautiful and helps her take on the spirit of Grace's enthusiastic post-mortems. She recalls feeling intimidated by it when she first stepped into the morgue, but she took it on as a fun challenge. She had never played a doctor before.

The actress also embraced the spirit of Ogden that was still very much in the walls. Much as Ogden was someone Grace admired, so too was Hélène Joy someone Georgina admired. Just as Ogden groomed Grace into the morgue, so did Hélène help groom Georgina onto the show. Some of the audience's favourite scenes involve the two women helping each other over a professional puzzle or a personal conundrum. The show and the morgue only benefitted from the introduction of another female character.

## DRESSING EMILY GRACE ✿✿✿✿✿✿✿✿✿✿✿✿✿✿✿✿✿✿✿✿✿✿✿✿✿✿✿✿✿✿✿✿✿✿✿✿✿✿✿✿✿✿✿✿

The biggest challenge Alex Reda and his team faced when Emily Grace was introduced was how to make her look different from Ogden, though their professions were the same. Alex was happy that Georgina looked so markedly different from Hélène, as the silhouette and colour choices would be automatically different for such a different woman. It was also helpful that Ogden would be moving into different stages of her career over the coming seasons, which gave Alex more freedom to make Ogden's fashion change, taking her character into an ever more distinct place from that of Emily Grace.

Alex chose to make Grace's clothing even more sensible than Ogden's. He used as his inspiration the rational dress movement, particularly the aims set out by the Rational Dress Society (est. 1881), a movement led by women who wanted their clothing to be more functional and less decorative, enabing them to move freely and go about their daily tasks without restrictions, as suits allowed men to. Alex took the male inspiration even further with Grace, dressing her in stiffer shirts with detachable collars, rather than soft blouses. He even went so far as to add cuff links, and continued on with neckties and waistcoats.

Grace's clothing also reflects a more subdued colour palette than Ogden, but with strong lines and silhouettes, so that when she removes her apron after a hard day of work, she looks smart and sexy, reflecting the way Grace is written and played.

Every so often Grace has a chance to put on a special gown. One of Georgina's favourite dresses is the pink chiffon gown she wore to the New Years' Eve ball at the end of season 5. It was such a departure from the masculine looks of Grace's everyday clothing that Georgina fell easily into the romance of the evening. This was exactly what Alex was hoping to achieve. A very feminine and soft colour palette shows another side of Grace outside of work, and places her in the higher social standing she now occupies. Long strands of pearls and layers of silk chiffon are used by Alex for Grace's evening looks to convey a very beautiful, confident woman in her element.

*An Alex Reda costume design for Grace.*

*Ogden and Grace inspect a portrait at an art gallery (611).*

*Grace recreates the victim's face (716).*

# FRIENDS
## and FOES

*"Be the man you were destined to be.*
*Holmes believed in logic, deduction, intellect.*
*And above all, the rule of law."*

Detective William Murdoch

*Previous spread: Sherlock Holmes (Andrew Gower) and Ben McQueen (Christian Distefano) (704).*

*This page: The cast and crew rehearse the brawl between the Toronto Constabulary and dockworkers on location at 270 Sherman in Hamilton (801).*

*Higgins (Lachlan Murdoch), Jackson (Kristian Bruun), Murdoch, Crabtree and the Toronto Constabulary head to the waterfront (801).*

# FRIENDS and FOES

Over the years Murdoch has met a great many people, typically through his investigations, who have left a lasting impression on both him and the audience. Some of these people are on Murdoch's side, and others staunchly against him. There are those characters we love to see return, to annoy or challenge Murdoch while he attempts to solve a case, to torment or punish him for perceived wrongs, or to support him in friendship. These characters enrich the world in which they all live, and the fictional world of Murdoch expands constantly to include them.

*Main: Murdoch is held back by Constable Higgins (Lachlan Murdoch) as his childhood friend Eddie Cullen runs into the burning barn (112).*

*Left: Higgins (Lachlan Murdoch) and Crabtree, after realizing that Brackenreid had given Murdoch the same bachelor party gift (803).*

# THE CONSTABLES

Police Station No. 4 doesn't run on just Brackenreid, Murdoch and Crabtree. There are always several constables in the background, interviewing witnesses, filing paperwork or typing up reports. A few of these constables are just as much a part of the station house family as the main characters, and the audience is equally invested in their antics.

*Murdoch gives the constables their marching orders to round up the anarchists (715).*

## CONSTABLE HENRY HIGGINS

Higgins, though of equal rank and experience to Crabtree, is always second choice to him in almost any task required by Murdoch or Brackenreid. Higgins genuinely tries hard to be good at his job, but simply isn't.

Higgins must notice that while he never quite understands what Murdoch is doing during the course of an investigation, Crabtree is quick-witted enough to follow along. Higgins is so in awe of Murdoch and his unconventional approach to policing, that it's all he can do to speak in Murdoch's presence, never mind admit he has no idea what Murdoch is talking about. With Brackenreid, actor Lachlan Murdoch always plays

Higgins as though he's hoping to stay out of Brackenreid's way. He feels as though Higgins is the one who catches Brackenreid's ire most of the time, and Higgins is only too aware of his place in Brackenreid's hierarchy.

### Higgins is Brackenreid's whipping boy.

Lachlan Murdoch, *Constable Henry Higgins*

He and Crabtree have an amusing and relatable relationship. Best friends who irritate each other, Higgins lives in jealousy of Crabtree's successes. Not only is Crabtree better at being a constable, but he is also more popular with the ladies and somehow taken seriously despite his endless supply of ridiculous theories. To Higgins, Crabtree's success is perplexing. After all, they have grown up on the job together. Higgins has great affection for his fellow constable, but can't help wondering what Crabtree has that he doesn't.

Every so often we hear a snippet of Higgins' love life. He makes himself out to be a bit of a heartbreaker, though just how much is true is a question that's not been answered so far. He even sets his eyes on Grace for a time, though it isn't clear how much is genuine attraction rather than one-upmanship with Crabtree. Murdoch set the precedent with Ogden, and if a lowly constable like Crabtree can land a smart, attractive lady of education and class, then why can't Higgins?

The comedic duo of Higgins and Crabtree are a fan favourite. Amongst cast and crew, when asked who their favourite onscreen couple is, Higgins and Crabtree were cited more often than any of the show's romantic pairings. Hélène Joy loves Crabtree and Higgins together because Higgins is a "constant curmudgeon, while Crabtree will believe in anything, but somehow Crabtree comes off as the smart one, until Higgins manages to turn the tables."

*Far left: Crabtree and Higgins (Lachlan Murdoch) find the murder weapon (612).*

*Left: Higgins (Lachlan Murdoch) watches as Murdoch interviews Fannie Robinson (Mariah Inger) about the death of her husband (103).*

*This page: Lachlan Murdoch and Jonny Harris show off their convincing post-explosion make-up (504).*

**Did You Know?**

Lachlan Murdoch originally auditioned for the role of Crabtree. The role eventually went to Jonny Harris, but the producers liked Lachlan so much they gave him a second constable role and thus Henry Higgins was born.

*Higgins (Lachlan Murdoch) and Jackson (Kristian Bruun) rejoice at their joint purchase of a car (805).*

*Grace, Jackson (Kristian Bruun) and Brackenreid enjoy the ride (805).*

*Constable Jackson (Kristian Bruun) faces off with a dockworker (801).*

Writer Paul Aitken has a fondness for writing Crabtree and Higgins together. To him, they are equals on the level of mutual respect, which allows them to talk about anything and everything. Higgins was created originally as a helping hand with constabulary duties and as a sounding board for Crabtree's various musings, but the character has grown over the years. Now Higgins functions primarily as a cynical counterweight to Crabtree's guileless optimism. Their conversations can be, almost simultaneously, magnificently stupid and astonishingly profound. Paul finds that these interactions can be valuable as a means by which a clue to the mystery can be hidden inside a seemingly random, and amusing, conversation.

Jonny Harris and Lachlan always enjoy their scenes together. Jonny finds it funny how Crabtree, who in many ways is the nicest guy in the world, always tends to get "flustered and pissy with Higgins." He blames it on "hereditary abuse. Crabtree catches hell from Brackenreid and passes it on to Higgins." Ultimately, though, Crabtree and Higgins are best friends. They squabble and fight, but in the end they are always there for one another.

Higgins works hard in Station No. 4. He might not always be the best constable, but he is one of the most dedicated, and we love watching him fumble through his tasks, revelling in satisfaction when he does something useful, and writhing in agony when he makes one of his classic mistakes.

## CONSTABLE SLUGGER JACKSON

Jackson makes his first appearance at Station No. 4 in season 5, as a rival constable at another station house. He is mistaken by Brackenreid for a ringer on Station No. 5's baseball team, and is consequently taken out of commission by a copious amount of alcohol and some well-timed slander against Jackson's wife.

Actor Kristian Bruun still recalls his audition clearly. He was a big fan of the show and had been dying to be cast in it, but as season 5 was in full swing, he had almost given up hope. Then his agent called him in for the part of Jackson, and Kristian clicked with it immediately. He was thrilled to be cast in what he expected would be just a two-episode arc. Little did he know that he would impress the producers with his period-perfect performance and be invited back to join Station No. 4 as a recurring constable.

Jackson is the third in line for Murdoch's assignments. If Crabtree is unavailable, Murdoch or Brackenreid will usually turn to Higgins. If Higgins is also otherwise engaged, then Jackson is called up to bat. Not so much a creative thinker, Jackson is the stereotypical period copper – solid and sturdy. He towers above the other constables

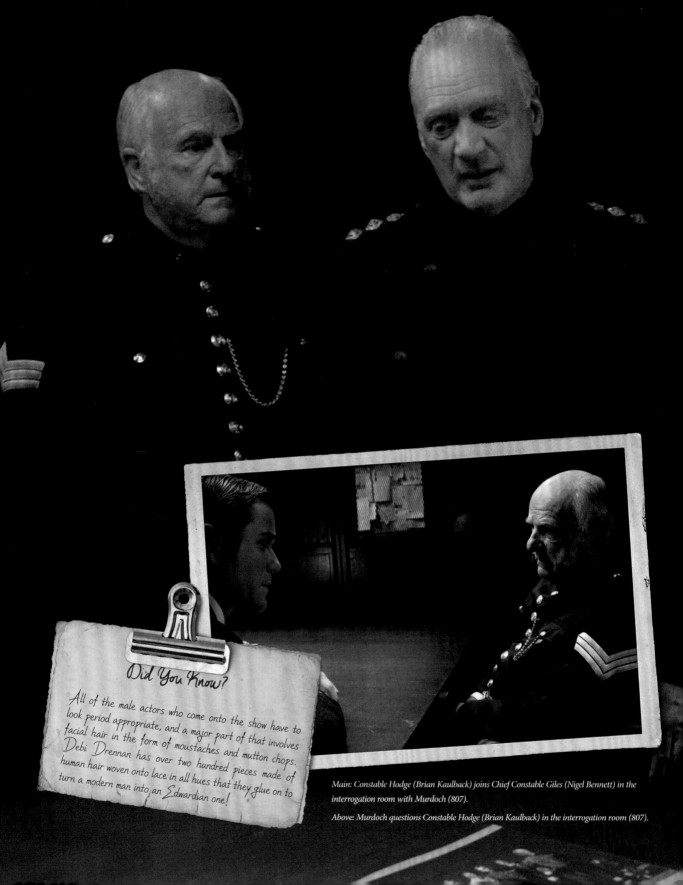

## Did You Know?

All of the male actors who come onto the show have to look period appropriate, and a major part of that involves facial hair in the form of moustaches and mutton chops. Debi Drennan has over two hundred pieces made of human hair woven onto lace in all hues that they glue on to turn a modern man into an Edwardian one!

*Main: Constable Hodge (Brian Kaulback) joins Chief Constable Giles (Nigel Bennett) in the interrogation room with Murdoch (807).*

*Above: Murdoch questions Constable Hodge (Brian Kaulback) in the interrogation room (807).*

in Station No. 4, and has no qualms about the use of violence in the course of his duty. However, Jackson is a study in contrasts. Loyal and kind, he can be very much the gentle giant with his friends, and will do whatever he is told without question. Like jumping off a moving car at Brackenreid's request, for example.

*My favourite episode was 'Murdoch au Naturel'. It was my favourite example of good writing, directing, acting, comedic timing, perfectly placed objects, how awkward the characters were around the naturists.*

Kristian Bruun, *Constable Slugger Jackson*

Kristian's favourite scenes to play are those in which Jackson, Higgins and Crabtree are all up to some scheme or another. The automobile the three purchase together is the perfect example of this. Three guys hanging out, much like the same three guys would hang out today, and getting into the same kind of trouble that guys have found themselves in throughout time.

Jackson has found a place at Station No. 4, and we're happy he is there to keep Toronto safe, even if it is one punch at a time.

## CONSTABLE JOHN HODGE

A fixture in Station No. 4 from the very beginning, Hodge, played by Brian Kaulback, was in the background of 103 episodes until his character took a dramatic turn. Hodge is a career constable, steady and dependable. When, in season 8, Murdoch reveals that Hodge killed a corrupt constable many years before to protect the reputation and honour of then-Detective Percival Giles, we see him for the loyal servant he is. The decision to take Hodge's character in that direction was not one entered into lightly. Great drama comes from emotional consequence, and though Hodge spent most of his time quietly in the background, he was still a familiar part of the station house.

Paul Aitken used Hodge and Giles as a parallel to Crabtree and Murdoch. Would Crabtree kill someone to protect Murdoch? If Hodge would for Giles, it is implied, then the answer is yes. Thus questions of loyalty and sacrifice ripple through Station No. 4. The situation presents Murdoch with a morally complex dilemma, but he must do his duty regardless, and Hodge knows this to be true. Hodge accepts the consequences of his actions with grace, and some relief. We hear his heartfelt confession, and watch the touching goodbye. Hodge may be gone, but he is not forgotten, and we may well learn what becomes of him in the future.

## CHIEF CONSTABLE PERCIVAL GILES ✦✦✦✦✦✦✦✦✦✦✦✦✦✦✦✦✦✦✦✦✦✦✦✦✦✦✦✦✦

We first meet Giles as an inspector at the end of season 4, called in to Station No. 4 to investigate a murder in which Murdoch is implicated. He is punctilious, rigid, humourless and difficult. He is also perceptive and clever, and a very good policeman. Which is why Murdoch ends up in the jail cells of Station No. 4, having been expertly framed by Constance Gardiner. Though eventually proven innocent, Murdoch suffers the consequences of that ordeal for years to come.

Giles accepts that Murdoch was framed by Constance Gardiner, but does not accept Brackenreid's explanation for her escape; that the cell door was broken, and she took advantage. The audience knows Brackenreid is not telling the whole truth, and so does Giles. Giles simply doesn't know why. This singular incident subsequently colours Giles' relationship with Station No. 4, as he is promoted to Chief Constable and makes it his mission to catch Murdoch out on that or any other lie. Giles knows Murdoch is an excellent detective, but he cannot abide circumvention of the law.

He enforces the law to its full extent when Ogden becomes the prime suspect in the murder of her husband, Darcy Garland, sending her to the noose. Though Murdoch manages to clear her name just in time.

While Giles has been almost a villain in the lives of our heroes, in season 8 we gain a whole new insight into his character, and we look at all of his past conduct in a new, softer, more understanding light. Though actor Nigel Bennett appreciates Giles' black-and-white attitude towards his work and enjoys playing the character's rigid sense of duty, when he was given the script for 'What Lies Buried', he was surprised, in the best way, that the show was choosing to deal with such a difficult topic. The historical context was a way of reflecting how far society has come since, yet how far it still has to progress. As Nigel says, "There are countries in the world now where being gay is a death sentence. I think that episode shows great courage from the producers."

It was a chance for Giles and Murdoch to be honest with one another, once and for all. Though both men follow the law, both have felt the need to contravene it for what is right, because what is right may not always be what is lawful. They may not like one another, but they certainly respect one another. Murdoch regrets ruining Giles' career, but in the case of murder, to which Giles is an accessory, he believes the law is right.

As for Giles' future, Nigel believes he'll be back. "They can't keep him in prison forever, and when he does return, he will be just as ornery, just as determined to do what is right, and just as irritatingly honest as he ever was."

*Inspector Giles forces Brackenreid out of Murdoch's interrogation. (413)*

*Chief Constable Giles (Nigel Bennett) at a hockey banquet (512)*

*Ogden is arrested for murder on Chief Constable Giles' (Nigel Bennett) order (512)*

## JAMES PENDRICK ❀❀❀❀❀❀❀❀❀❀❀❀❀❀❀❀❀❀❀❀❀❀❀❀❀❀❀❀❀❀❀❀❀❀❀❀❀❀❀❀❀

When James Pendrick was introduced in season 3, it was with a very specific idea in mind. The writers had created Pendrick to be Murdoch's nemesis. However, before they wrote the first episode in which the character was to appear, the decision was made to throw the audience the ultimate twist. Although Pendrick would seem by all accounts to be guilty, the real villain would be his wife, Sally. Interestingly, the writers chose to keep the exact same personality for James Pendrick that they had constructed, though he would no longer to be a villain.

Writer Carol Hay describes the dashing, witty and rich James Pendrick as Murdoch's intellectual equal – both of them sharing an interest in the scientific future. Yet from the get-go, Murdoch distrusts him, an opinion that Pendrick's superior "above the law" demeanour does nothing to dispel.

Actor Peter Stebbings enjoys Pendrick's devil-may-care attitude. He recalls that on his first day on set, Cal Coons took him aside and explained the show doesn't take itself too seriously, and neither should Pendrick. Stebbings consequently created the dashing Pendrick we love to see appear each season, playing him as a "debonaire, swashbuckling scientist-inventor-millionaire, with a dash of arrogance," taking his cue from the imaginative and forward-thinking schemes Pendrick is always hatching.

*James Pendrick (Peter Stebbings) and his wife Sally (Kate Greenhouse) unveil a Rembrandt painting (306).*

*Main: James Pendrick (Peter Stebbings) leads a meeting of the Toronto Eugenics Society (308).*

*Below: Jonny Harris, Peter Stebbings and Yannick Bisson relax between takes (703).*

*James Pendrick (Peter Stebbings) and Murdoch climb into the plane (601).*

*Below: Rob Carli's score for the key moment in the episode, 'Flying The Plane' (601).*

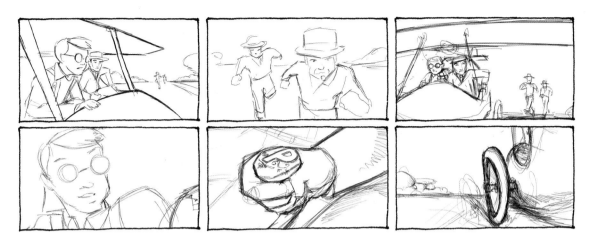

*Storyboards for the takeoff.*

Yannick Bisson always enjoys the episodes in which Pendrick appears. The meeting of minds is fun for him to play, and he is always intrigued by Pendrick's latest scheme. As Yannick says, "Who else could have brought a film crew to Station No. 4 or contrived to race his electric car against Henry Ford?"

Pendrick's character does have a near-fatal flaw, though. He is almost too far ahead of his time – his revolutionary ideas forever being manipulated by others for less than pure intentions. From skyscrapers to cars to airplanes to moving pictures, Pendrick is nevertheless indefatigable in his desire to contribute to the betterment of humanity. Though he has yet to succeed at any of his ventures, his pioneer spirit is undimmed. We wait in anticipation of what amazing modern invention Pendrick thinks of next.

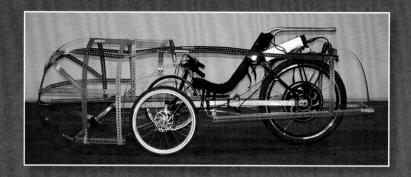

# THE ELECTRIC CAR

When Craig Grant was approached to build an electric car that needed to look unlike anything anyone had seen before, he found himself unusually stumped. He tinkered with a few ideas and looked for period-accurate cars to purchase or emulate, but nothing seemed quite right for the story or for Pendrick. Then, while driving to set in Port Hope, Ontario, Craig noted an enclosed carrying case on another car. The shape was sleek, the materials workable, and the price affordable. He had the design for his electric car.

It took two weeks to source the largest car case in Toronto, which he then placed over a three-wheel recumbent bicycle. He fitted out the bike with a 48-volt motor and rigged up the steering and controls, with the whole process taking about four months. Normally Craig has about two weeks to design and build whatever invention the writers come up with. In this case, the car would be the centrepiece of the episode, so it had to be exceptional.

Once built, Craig test drove it up and down the road outside the Murdoch studio. Neighbouring businesses were somewhat perplexed at the sight, while the crew enjoyed watching Craig take the car up to as fast as forty-five kilometres per hour. It crashed twice, once with Craig inside, and once with Yannick at the wheel. Craig recalls how the car rolled over with Yannick still inside. He was unhurt, luckily, but stuck, so the crew had to lift the car back upright with Yannick still in the driver's seat!

Peter Stebbings remembers whipping around in the car for the episode. "It was really fun to drive, and gave new meaning to 'action'!" He was very impressed, as was the rest of cast and crew, that Craig managed to build an actual working electric car from scratch. Not only did the car work as a futuristic take from an 1899 perspective, but it also worked as the kind of car Pendrick would imagine. Perhaps most importantly, it worked for the production, as the actors could safely drive the car themselves without the need for stunt doubles, so the camera could catch both Murdoch and Pendrick's delighted faces as they took Craig's pride and joy out on the open roads of Victorian Toronto.

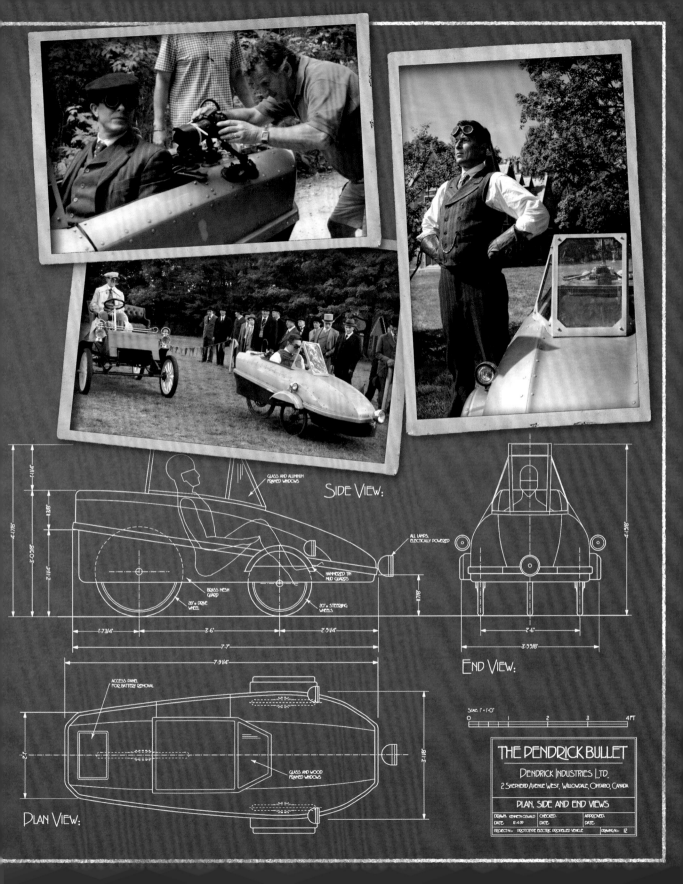

SIDE VIEW:

GLASS AND ALUMINIUM
FRAMED WINDOWS

ALL LAMPS
ELECTRICALLY POWERED

HAMMERED TIN
MUD GUARDS

BRASS MESH
GUARD

28" ⌀ DRIVE
WHEEL

20" ⌀ STEERING
WHEELS

END VIEW:

ACCESS PANEL
FOR BATTERY REMOVAL

GLASS AND WOOD
FRAMED WINDOWS

PLAN VIEW:

SCALE: 1" = 1'-0"

0        1        2        3        4 FT

## THE PENDRICK BULLET

PENDRICK INDUSTRIES LTD.

2 SHEPHERD AVENUE WEST, WILLOWDALE, ONTARIO, CANADA

PLAN, SIDE AND END VIEWS

| DRAWN: KENNETH OSWALD | CHECKED: | APPROVED: |
| DATE: 12-4-59 | DATE: | DATE: |
| PROJECT NO: PROTOTYPE ELECTRIC PROPELLED VEHICLE | | DRAWING NO: 12 |

*Yannick Bisson, Peter Keleghan (Terrence Meyers)*
*and Thomas Craig relax between takes (715)*

## Did You Know?

Peter Keleghan was filming a scene which required him to wield a real firearm, loaded with blanks, when former-Ontario Lieutenant Governor David Onley was visiting the set. Between set-ups, Peter went to greet him. "It didn't take long for the props guy to register the look on his security guards' faces as I quickly walked toward him." He handed the props gun back

## TERRENCE MEYERS ✳✳✳✳✳✳✳✳✳✳✳✳✳✳✳✳✳✳✳✳✳✳✳✳✳✳✳✳✳✳✳✳✳✳✳✳✳✳✳✳✳✳

Meyers first appears in season 1 as a seemingly innocent land developer, later revealed to be a spy involved in the manufacture of a war machine. As a Canadian spy, we assume he must be a good character, but his actions speak otherwise. Meyers is dedicated to his work and will do whatever it takes to complete his missions, with little to no regard for the human lives affected. Naturally, therefore, when he first meets Murdoch, Meyers considers him just as expendable as the average citizen, but after seeing Murdoch's knack for solving a mystery, Meyers begins to use the detective to his advantage. Year after year the audience squirms with delight when Meyers magically appears in the middle of Murdoch's investigations, knowing Murdoch is in for unending lies and frustration while Meyers manipulates everything he can for his own top-secret purposes. The truth according to Meyers has many different variations, depending on what he needs the truth to be at any given moment. His catchphrase, "It's a matter of national security," is used to cover anything and everything he does not himself know or doesn't want to share.

Cal Coons relished the idea of the first Canadian spy. He loved the thought of straight-laced Murdoch being thrown into this world of deception and intrigue, about as far as possible from his own organized and methodical way of life. Similarly, actor Peter Keleghan loves the ambiguity of the character. No one can ever be sure of Meyers' true agenda, and his duplicity is enjoyable to play, especially as that duplicity is in such stark contrast to Murdoch and his colleagues at Station No. 4. Peter is also partial to the moment in each Meyers episode where he and Murdoch meet for the first time. "Murdoch is, justifiably, wearily resigned to his appearance and the new adventure," he says, "and in the end is equally justified shaking his head at what just happened."

Murdoch often finds Meyers at the heart of the biggest cases he investigates, frequently those involving other countries and, in particular, the United States of America. The Americans have their own version of Meyers in the form of Allen Clegg, and Murdoch tends to find himself stuck in the middle of these two duplicitous gentlemen's espionage activities, and is forced to spend a large part of his investigation simply trying to extricate himself from the complex web of lies and intrigue the two rival spies spin at each other.

## ALLEN CLEGG ✳✳✳✳✳✳✳✳✳✳✳✳✳✳✳✳✳✳✳✳✳✳✳✳✳✳✳✳✳✳✳✳✳✳✳✳✳✳✳✳✳✳✳✳✳✳

Clegg is the American version of Meyers, only without the latter's sense of humour. Where Meyers appears to enormously enjoy the spy racket, Clegg takes it all very seriously. The two rivals will do anything to best the other, including sacrificing the lives of innocent bystanders, and neither has any qualms about engineering the demise of the other. When Clegg frames Meyers for the assassination of President McKinley, it is only because of Murdoch's tenacity and creative thinking that Meyers is ultimately exonerated. Clegg scowls at the failure of what would have been his ultimate triumph, while Meyers – never one to hold a grudge – finds the whole escapade highly amusing.

Clegg has no love for Murdoch, but, like Meyers, will use the detective to his advantage when he has the opportunity. Murdoch, naturally, is well aware he is constantly being manipulated, and will only play along when it helps him find a murderer, or the truth.

Clegg is both friend and foe, and not the best ambassador for the US in Canada, though whether he truly represents the interests of the American government is somewhat up for debate. He certainly represents deception, and serves as a reminder of the dangerous delicacy of the longest undefended border in the world.

## ANNA FULFORD

Initially, Anna is everything Julia Ogden is not. Anna is working class and knows it. Though she would love adventure and travel, she has no choice but to work for her living.

Meeting Murdoch, even without his memories, opens up a realm of possibilities for Anna. She realizes that there are men of culture and intelligence in the world who are not concerned with class or wealth. She sees the potential for a life outside of the pub in Bristol, and sets about making it happen. She can't help but be attracted to Murdoch, the lost soul in need of help, and her kindness attracts Murdoch in turn. But his heart belongs to another, and though tempted, he can't bring himself to leave his life in Toronto for Anna.

Murdoch and Anna are reunited when her fiancé is killed by the nefarious Black Hand, during the period when Ogden is engaged to Darcy. Romance isn't high on the list of priorities while Murdoch investigates Anna's fiancé's murder, but a small spark does begin to glow between them. When Anna takes her life into her own hands by returning to Toronto, in season 5, that spark grows into a flame, and we believe Murdoch may really be ready to move on from the now-married Ogden with Anna.

Anna brings out a more casual side of Murdoch. Not one for lengthy discussions on science or medicine, he and Anna are comfortable together. Some fans prefer this version of Murdoch to how he is with Ogden, and like that Anna isn't shy to share her feelings. It is true that Murdoch develops a deep fondness for Anna, and is perhaps regretful that they are forced apart by the Black Hand. Ultimately, though, deep in his heart, Ogden is the one, and Anna knows this, too.

*Above: Yannick Bisson signs autographs for fans between takes.*

*Main: Anna Fulford (Lisa Faulkner) and Murdoch (507).*

*When shooting in public places, Yannick Bisson and the other actors will always take the time (barring severe time constraints) to acknowledge and/or gleefully mingle and chat with the gathered crowds or a single person, to give them, the loyal viewers, the respect they deserve. I think this plays a huge part in why the show is so successful and has been for so many seasons!*

Yuri Yakubiw, *Director of Photography*

Despite the fact that psychology in the 1890s was still an emerging and largely unproven field, Murdoch finds consulting radical psychiatrist Dr Roberts helpful in several of his cases. Having been relieved of his duties at the Provincial Lunatic Asylum because of his radical techniques (a post he would later regain), Ogden first refers Murdoch to him to help create a psychological profile of a serial killer – all very unusual and quite groundbreaking! Ogden finds Dr Roberts equally helpful in ridding herself of the night terrors brought on by her burial at the hands of James Gillies. It is through this experience that Ogden begins her fascination with psychology, having felt its benefits for herself.

Dr Roberts meets a tragic end when diagnosis of his terminal illness drives him towards an extreme decision. He is immersed in liquid nitrogen, frozen, in the hopes of a cure in the distant future. Ogden is saddened and fascinated by his final act. She can't return to the morgue, and her private practice has been disrupted by her illegal teachings. She realizes she has found her new calling. Psychiatry is a new field full of possibility and exploration. A new start for a new century. She has Dr Roberts to thank for opening her eyes to this fledgling and exciting field of medicine.

## CK HOLMES ✦✦✦✦✦✦✦✦✦✦✦✦✦✦✦✦✦✦✦✦✦✦✦✦✦✦✦✦✦✦✦✦✦✦✦✦✦

A fictional character from outside the (fictional) world of *Murdoch Mysteries* had never before been written into the show as a 'live' character before. Thus, there was some confusion amongst fans when it was announced that Murdoch would solve a case with Sherlock Holmes, the legendary detective of Victorian literature. Adding to the confusion was the fact that Holmes' creator, Sir Arthur Conan Doyle, had already appeared as a character on the show twice.

However, in true Murdochian fashion, the Sherlock Holmes solving crimes in Victorian Toronto actually turns out to be a young man named David Kingsley, in the throes of a psychotic break where his mind was only able to cope with reality by assuming the identity of the fictional detective. Audiences heaved a sigh of relief. The writers had not completely lost their minds, and we were all free to enjoy the two episodes in which "Sherlock" appeared.

David Kingsley and his father enjoyed a mutual love of literature and of Sherlock Holmes in particular. In assuming Sherlock's identity, Kingsley was able to deal with the trauma of his father's murder, and prove himself a worthy detective in his own right. Much to Murdoch's annoyance, Sherlock managed to stay one step ahead of him

*Dr. Roberts hypnotizes Charlotte Taylor in an attempt to interview her other two personalities about the murder of her father (305).*

throughout the investigation. Of course, it wasn't all fair given that Sherlock had insider knowledge of the crime, albeit buried deep in his psyche. Still, Kingsley discovers an aptitude for detecting and sets up his own private detective agency in Toronto. Though he can't quite seem to rid himself of the deerstalker and tweed cape, even after he regains his true identity. Kingsley is more helpful the second time Murdoch's path crosses his, but there is already a great detective in Toronto, and his name is William Murdoch.

*Sherlock Holmes (Andrew Gower) finds missing nanny Nora (Emily Klassen), in disguise as a boy, with Brackenreid (704).*

## ISAAC TASH

Through meeting Isaac Tash in season 1, we learn about Ogden's life before the morgue. She and Tash studied medicine together at Bishop's University and we are given the impression Tash and Ogden have a history. Though Tash is nothing but kind with Murdoch, his presence allows the audience to catch a glimpse of the passion welling in Murdoch's heart for Ogden. His affection for her and jealousy of Tash apparent, Murdoch asks Ogden if she and Tash had courted, but Ogden brushes off the question.

Thus, when Tash appears again in season 2 in connection with abortions, Murdoch cannot help but believe the worst – that Tash was the father of Ogden's unwanted child. Blighted by jealousy, Murdoch is not as his most impartial as he works through the case, and only restrains himself from arresting Tash because of the distress and ruin it would cause his patients. The first major blow to their fledgling relationship, Murdoch feels betrayed by Ogden's past, and how it could affect their future together. Ogden is angry with Murdoch for refusing to consider the issue of abortion less rigidly, and for attacking Tash. Though illegally terminating pregnancies, Tash was doing so safely and professionally.

Tash becomes the catalyst for this seemingly insurmountable obstacle to Murdoch and Ogden's happiness that will linger between them for some time to come.

*Inadvertently, Isaac Tash (Steven McCarthy) and Ogden are caught in a friendly embrace (206).*

Main: Sally Pendrick (Kate Greenhouse) attends a Toronto Eugenics Society meeting with her husband (308).

Left: Cornered, Sally Pendrick (Kate Greenhouse) fires back and makes a run for it (313).

## CONSTANCE GARDINER ✵✵✵✵✵✵✵✵✵✵✵✵✵✵✵✵✵✵✵✵✵✵✵✵✵✵✵✵✵✵✵✵✵✵✵✵✵✵✵✵✵✵✵✵✵✵

Constance Gardiner, aka Ava Moon, affects the lives of *Murdoch Mysteries'* main characters in more ways than one. Having been brutally assaulted and left physically and emotionally scarred several years before we meet her in the show, she has plotted her revenge against her attacker carefully.

Then-Constable Murdoch had convinced her to testify against Michael Cudmore as a witness to another crime. Cudmore confessed, 'persuaded' by the bloodied knuckles of Murdoch's inspector, so when called upon in court, Murdoch conscientiously testified that the confession was not given voluntarily, and the case was dimissed. Freed, Cudmore took his revenge on Constance by ruining her face and her life.

When Murdoch walks in to the Lewis Caroll party in the season 4 finale where Constance is about to exact her revenge, she can't help but involve him in her plans. She kills Cudmore and frames Murdoch. He in turn, acknowledging the part he had to play in the whole affair, chooses justice over the law and releases her from jail. In so doing, Murdoch loses his chance to prevent Ogden from marrying Darcy. In a way, Murdoch prescribes his own penance. In saving Constance Gardiner he consciously ruins any chance he may have had at happiness with Ogden. He also puts his career in jeopardy, compromises his boss and friend Brackenreid, and makes an adversary of then-Inspector Percival Giles.

The effects of Murdoch's decision rattle the foundations of the show, and ripple through the years. Only in season 8 is it finally put to rest as Murdoch and Ogden marry, and Giles, in no position to do anything about it, is granted the whole truth.

## SALLY PENDRICK ✵✵✵✵✵✵✵✵✵✵✵✵✵✵✵✵✵✵✵✵✵✵✵✵✵✵✵✵✵✵✵✵✵✵✵✵✵✵✵✵✵✵✵✵✵✵✵✵

Originally Sally Pendrick was conceived as a kind of nouveau riche bohemian who would tempt Murdoch and push him out of his comfortable understanding with Ogden in season 3. Then, as the writers worked through the storylines, they realized that she would make a much more interesting villain, and an unexpected one at that.

Unconventional, ostentatious and uninhibited, Sally Pendrick stands out in Toronto society. Where Ogden would rely on logic and intelligence to achieve her goals, Sally Pendrick flaunts her wealth and feminine assets. Murdoch has some difficulty dealing with such an overtly sexualized woman, and as his investigations return again and again to her husband James, he begins to worry for her safety. Capitalizing on Murdoch's manly instinct to protect her, Sally feeds into his suspicions of her husband, manipulating events to place James Pendrick more and more directly in the frame. Murdoch realizes almost

*Main: Dr Darcy Garland (Jonathan Watton) arrives at Ogden's office (607).*

*Right top: Dr Lawrence Abbot (Stewart Arnott), Dr Martin Falwell (Kevin Bundy) and Dr Darcy Garland (Jonathan Watton) with a patient (Mikaela Bisson) (403).*

*Right: Murdoch dreams of an encounter between him and Eva Pearce (Daiva Johnston-Zalnieriunas) (608).*

too late that he has been fooled, and despite his best efforts, Sally Pendrick escapes his grasp. A murderer and a con artist, she knows better than to return to Toronto. In Murdoch she had finally met her match, and Murdoch learns that women have just as great a capacity for evil as men.

## EVA PEARCE

Sally Pendrick is not the only woman to pull the wool over Murdoch's eyes. Eva Pearce, a shopgirl at Eaton's, may not be quite on Sally's level – her scams mainly involve leeching off of wealthy men – but so overpowering is her desire for wealth and status that she will resort to any means to land a rich husband. Even murder.

Young and beautiful, though Murdoch eventually entraps her, Eva still wields tremendous power over other men, managing to escape the noose for her crimes and be instead admitted to Ogden's asylum. There a new plan is set in motion, and Eva uses Ogden and Murdoch to her advantage and secures her freedom. But Eva may have gone too far. In feigning insanity she may well have truly lost her grip on reality. She appears to believe Murdoch is in love with her, and Ogden is the enemy. Eva may have freed herself from her cell, but she has yet to free Murdoch from his shackles – Ogden.

## DARCY GARLAND

Dr Darcy Garland was working at the Buffalo Hospital for Sick Children when Julia Ogden arrived. He was instantly taken with her charm and grace, but more with her talent and drive. She is an extraordinary woman, and Darcy is utterly beguiled by her. On Ogden's part, Darcy represents everything she should want in a husband. Kind, educated, professional, from a good family and of good standing, he is an ideal match.

When Ogden arrives in Buffalo, she believes Murdoch has no interest in continuing their relationship. They are at the point in their saga where her inability to have children has become a wall between them, and they are both incapable of talking their way around the matter. Darcy presents a solution. We can imagine her relief as he courts her, with no expectations contrary to what she can offer him, and the ease of their courtship becomes a balm to her broken heart.

Of course Ogden's place is in Toronto, and she dearly misses the morgue and her independence in her work. Her return to the city is somewhat awkward, though not for Darcy, who remains blissfully unaware of Murdoch and Ogden's history until just before their wedding. When he finds out, though, he heads directly to Murdoch's office. In this confrontation we see how much Darcy truly loves Ogden. He is a good man, and he would do anything for her. It isn't his fault that things go awry. He simply isn't William Murdoch.

The marriage disintegrates on several fronts. Not only is Ogden pursuing her illegal birth control clinic, but her dissatisfaction with her marriage makes her reluctant to tow the party line and play the dutiful wife with Darcy's superiors. Darcy realizes the futility of the situation and gives Ogden the freedom to leave him. He even consents to an annulment, and then a divorce, despite the consequences he will have to suffer in his public life. However, something changes for Darcy. He has been kind and understanding throughout the ordeal, but perhaps he begins to feel Ogden has not had to suffer for her actions. After all, she toyed with his affections and has impacted his career. So he uses what power he has in petty revenge by changing his mind and refusing to divorce Ogden.

Darcy subsequently comes to a tragic end, killed by James Gillies as part of a plan for revenge on Murdoch when Darcy's refusal to divorce supplied Gillies with the perfect motive to use in framing Ogden for murder. Darcy's death consequently mars Murdoch and Ogden's happiness for some time to come.

## LESLIE GARLAND

Leslie appears in season 7 innocently enough as the bereaved brother-in-law to Ogden, hoping to start his life fresh in the city that claimed his brother only a few months before. So, did he actually come to Toronto with a fully formed plan for revenge? Actor Giacomo Gianniotti believes not, feeling that Leslie had no real plan when he first arrived, but after seeing Ogden so happy with Murdoch, seemingly without a thought for the death of his brother that allowed for her freedom, he was spurred into action.

When he spies an opportunity to give Ogden her comeuppance, after the supposed death of James Gillies, he seizes it. Obtaining information on Gillies is simple enough, and planting the letter and evidence to torment Ogden and deprive her of her love is even easier. However, Leslie is no evil mastermind. He didn't plan for the eventuality that Ogden would tell Murdoch, or that Gillies' body would be discovered, and that the trail would inevitably lead back to him. Ultimately, though, it seems he doesn't care. Perhaps some part of him hoped to be discovered so he could stop playing the part of loving brother-in-law to a woman he had come to detest.

Leslie would likely have been completely satisfied with the results of his scheme, had it not been for the one person he wishes to keep in his life, but is now another on his long list of enemies. When Leslie spies Grace on the beach with Crabtree, he has no idea of

Leslie Garland (Giacomo Gianniotti), about to ask Dr Grace on a date (712).

## Did You Know?

Giacomo Gianniotti auditioned for Leslie Garland in his jeans and T-shirt and didn't get so much as a callback. When he went in to audition as one of the cyclists in 'Tour de Murdoch', he wore a suit, was immediately asked to re-read Leslie, and was cast right after that!

Leslie Garland (Giacomo Gianniotti) speaks to Ogden (802).

*James Gillies (Michael Seater) is concerned about the lecture Murdoch is giving his Physics class (207).*

**Did You Know?**

If you listen closely you'll hear the similarities between the theme music that accompanies James Gillies and that which accompanies Murdoch. Rob Carli calls it a perversion of Murdoch's theme, and if you think about it, Gillies character can be called a perversion of Murdoch's. If the music fits...

*Using physics, James Gillies (Michael Seater), Murdoch, Crabtree and Robert Perry (Marc Bendavid) prove where the bullet was fired from (207).*

her connection to Ogden and Murdoch. He simply sees a beautiful woman, and feels an instant attraction to her. He pursues her, even after he learns she is courting Constable Crabtree, Murdoch's right-hand man. In fact, that makes Grace more of a prize. Leslie turns on his considerable charm, driving a wedge between Crabtree and Grace and ultimately winning her. His victory is short-lived, however, as the truth of his actions against Ogden come out, and Grace's reaction cannot be mistaken.

For the *Murdoch Mysteries* audience, Leslie is a character they love to hate. He is young and charismatic, and insinuates himself into everyone's lives, while viewers can see the malevolent gleam in his eye. Giacomo also thoroughly enjoys playing a bad character and was thrilled when one fan commented that they "hate Leslie Garland. The only garland I want to see is one around his neck at the bottom of Lake Ontario!" After all, it's a big compliment to play a villain so well the audience wants your character dead!

Despite the universal dislike for Leslie Garland – on and off screen – Leslie chooses to stay in Toronto. He finishes his law degree and begins working under the Crown Attorney. When his attempt to reingratiate himself by offering to free Grace and Ogden from the charges brought against them after demonstrating for women's suffrage fails, Leslie instead manipulates Grace's prosecution to produce a trumped-up charge. Once again, his plans are foiled by Ogden, but now that Leslie has joined the legal profession, he might not be so easy to defeat in the future.

## JAMES GILLIES

Ah, Gillies. From such humble beginnings springs such great evil. When James Gillies was originally conceived in season 2, it was in tandem with another character, Robert Perry – a take on the infamous real-life crime duo of Nathan Leopold and Richard Loeb who murdered a teenage boy in 1924. No one expected he would return three years later, and with a vengeance.

*There is a great camaraderie amongst the cast and crew.*
*Working on* Murdoch *is like hanging out with friends solving murders.*

Michael Seater, *James Gillies*

In season 5 the writers wanted to introduce an arch-nemesis for Murdoch. There had been enemies to Murdoch on the show before, like Sally Pendrick, but there was room for a character who would want to exact revenge on Murdoch, and who had the intelligence to match, if not surpass, Murdoch's own skills. When the writing room looked back

hrough past seasons, one character stood out. James Gillies. He was a sociopath, given that the murder at his university was designed purely as an experiment. He immensely enjoyed watching Murdoch investigate, and was a bit of a poor sport when he was caught. We can imagine that Gillies' wealthy family hired the best barristers, keeping him from the gallows, and that he spent most of his considerable free time in jail plotting how he would not only beat Murdoch at his own game, but make him suffer in the process.

So Gillies becomes Murdoch's ultimate foe. The match of wits, with Gillies always one step ahead, and with the deadliest of consequences, always makes for thrilling and terrifying encounters between the two men. Actor Michael Seater enjoyed the change from curious sociopathic school boy to vengeful psychopathic lunatic. He loves how Gillies has become openly despicable and overtly evil. He is still amazed how much impact the character of Gillies has had on the audience, recalling several times being approached by fans on the street who don't hesitate to tell Michael how much they love to hate him.

Gillies has also had an enormous impact onscreen. Not only is he Murdoch's nemesis but also his tormentor, and after season 5 he becomes a constant threat to Murdoch and Ogden's lives. Though it can be argued that Gillies is the architect of Murdoch and Ogden's ultimate happiness, he causes them enormous suffering along the way, murdering Darcy and framing Ogden, all for his own perverse experiment. Gillies, incapable of emotion himself, knows Murdoch will sacrifice himself to save Ogden's life if necessary, and he relishes every moment of Murdoch's struggle before then. He wields tremendous psychological power over Murdoch and Ogden, and by extension Brackenreid and all of the constants of Station No. 4. Gillies enjoys watching everyone tiptoe around him, knowing he can manipulate events to his advantage and secure his escape.

James Gillies (Michael Seater) describes his plan for Murdoch (613).

Did You Know?

No matter how many times Michael Seater asks, no one will tell him if James Gillies is really dead...

Murdoch offers payback to James Gillies (Michael Seater) (709).

# Historical
# CHARACTERS

Jack London *"It's London, Jack London. And what was that you said? The call of the…"*

Detective William Murdoch *"Call of the wild."*

London *"That's a nice turn of phrase."*

*Previous spread: Murdoch and Jack London (Aaron Ashmore) in the Klondike countryside, beside the Yukon River (501).*

*Main: Alexander Graham Bell (John Tench) and Murdoch use the audiograph to analyze a speech (509).*

*Left: Fire threatens Murdoch and Prince Alfred (Chad Connell) (112).*

# Historical CHARACTERS

Part of the charm of *Murdoch Mysteries* lies in its references to real persons and events familiar to the audience. When historical figures visit the fictional world of Murdoch, it always means a delightful twist on their contributions to history. As a result, Murdoch and the other lead characters have often been the inspirations for scientific breakthroughs, modern inventions or famous novels. After all, these ideas all had to come from somewhere, so why not from Murdoch himself!

**Prince Alfred** (1844-1900), Duke of Saxe-Coburg and Gotha, was the second son and fourth child of Queen Victoria of the United Kingdom of Great Britain and Ireland and Prince Albert of Saxe-Coburg and Gotha. Appears in season 1 episode 12 [112].

Though in Toronto on official business, Prince Alfred is more interested in enjoying himself and Crabtree can barely keep the prince in his sights, despite a very real Fenian threat against him. He buys Crabtree a dandy of a suit, and allows Higgins to wear his royal uniform as his undercover double. The prince is kidnapped nonetheless, and Murdoch with him. Murdoch entreats one of the Fenians, his childhood friend, to spare them and the assassination attempt is thwarted.

**Alexander Graham Bell** (1847-1922) was a Scottish-born inventor, engineer and scientist credited with the invention of the telephone. 509, 511.

Murdoch meets Bell under unfortunate circumstances. His inventions are on display at an invention convention, where one of his fellow inventors is murdered. Murdoch, to his dismay, must treat Bell as a suspect, but before long the inventor becomes helpful in solving the murder. Months later, when Ogden is kidnapped by the evil James Gillies, Murdoch turns to Bell and his cutting-edge sound technology to help determine where she is being kept. Without Bell, Murdoch may never have found her, and our two favourite lovers would have been kept apart for eternity.

*The Black Hand* was an extortion racket that operated within the Italian immigrant community in major American cities. 409, 507, 508.

When the Black Hand extends its illegal empire to Toronto, Anna Fulford becomes an unknowing witness to their nefarious activities. Murdoch saves her once, and again from being silenced forever by these dangerous and powerful men.

*Brackenreid meets Andrew Carnegie (Philip Craig) at a ribbon-cutting ceremony (713).*

*Brackenreid flirts with Cassie Chadwick (Wendy Crewson) (713).*

*Andrew Carnegie* (1835-1919) was a Scottish-born American industrialist and philanthropist. 713.

Carnegie donated funds across North America to open libraries meant to be free to the public, many of which still stand in Toronto and southern Ontario today. On one such trip to Toronto, he discovers that a woman named Cassie Chadwick is claiming to be his daughter. Knowing of no such person, Carnegie unwittingly helps Murdoch catch Eva Pearce, masquerading as Cassie Chadwick.

*Cassie Chadwick*, born Elizabeth Bigley (1857-1907), was a Canadian fraudster who claimed to be Andrew Carnegie's heir and cheated American banks out of millions of dollars. 713.

In Toronto, because Eva Pearce is ruining her lucrative Carnegie scheme by assuming it herself, Chadwick turns Brackenreid's head with her well-rehearsed charm. She helps Murdoch catch Eva Pearce once and for all, reclaiming her Carnegie scam and leaving Murdoch and Brackenreid feeling somewhat foolish.

*Winston Churchill* (1874-1965) was a British soldier, writer, artist and politician who rose to become Prime Minister of the United Kingdom 1940-1945 and 1951-1955. 602.

*Main: Winston Churchill (Thomas Howes) and Murdoch glean a clue about the night before from the newspaper (602).*

*Right: Jeff Lillico (Reginald Mayfair) and Thomas Howes (Winston Churchill) discuss a scene at the speakeasy with director Don McCutcheon (602).*

*Main: Murdoch's admirer, Sir Arthur Conan Doyle (Geraint Wyn Davies) (104).*

*Left: Buffalo Bill (Nicholas Campbell) rides into the Wild Wild West show (201).*

In Toronto in 1900 on a lecture tour, Churchill is the toast of Toronto society. But he hadn't anticipated the murder of a friend and the resultant blood all over his hands. With memories of the night before a bit foggy, Murdoch helps him to retrace his steps, revealing both Churchill as a young man and the Churchill to come. Murdoch exonerates him and saves his life, ensuring Churchill can fulfill his destiny in the great wars to come.

Dr Daniel Clark (1830-1912) was a Scottish-born Canadian publisher, author, physician and medical superintendent of the Provincial Lunatic Asylum in Toronto, Ontario, 1875-1905. 612, 613, 706.

William Frederick "Buffalo Bill" Cody (1846-1917), whose father was Canadian, was an American soldier, scout, hunter and showman. 201.

Buffalo Bill's Wild West show (est. 1883) toured North America and Europe for decades, and was the highlight of any town it rolled into. Such was the case in Toronto, though the show quickly turns to tragedy when one of the performers is killed right in front of the audience. Buffalo Bill is forever grateful to Murdoch for solving the case and outing the murderer, and his show lives on to play another day.

George Dixon (1870-1908), aka Little Chocolate, was the first black Canadian boxer and the first Canadian, and black, world boxing champion 1890. 803.

Dr Perry E. Doolittle (1861-1933) was a co-founder of the Toronto Automobile Club (est. 1913), the founder of the Trans-Canada Highway, purchaser of the first used car in Canada in 1899, and the first Canadian to drive from Halifax to Vancouver in 1925. 805.

Arthur Conan Doyle (1859-1930) was a Scottish writer and physician and the creator of the fictional detective Sherlock Holmes. 104, 109, 604.

When Doyle appears in Toronto, it is after he has killed Sherlock Holmes by throwing him off the Reichenbach Falls in 'The Final Problem' (1893), apparently ending the very popular series of stories about the quintessential Victorian detective. However, while watching Murdoch solve a murder to which Doyle was a witness, Brackenreid pitches him his next story – "Hellhound of the Highlands" (the inspiration for *The Hound of the Baskervilles*). Several years later, Sherlock Holmes himself apparently springs to life in Toronto, and Arthur Conan Doyle comes to meet his creation in the flesh, learning exactly how to resurrect his fictional Sherlock from the dead in the process. So if it wasn't for Station No. 4, Conan Doyle may never have figured out how to continue Sherlock's adventures.

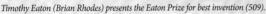

*Timothy Eaton (Brian Rhodes) presents the Eaton Prize for best invention (509).*   *Store owner John Craig Eaton (Michael Therriault) with Brackenreid (608).*

**John Craig Eaton** (1876-1922), the son of Timothy Eaton, was a businessman and philanthropist. 608.

Taken in by temptress Eva Pearce, John almost marries his Eaton inheritance to a con woman. Thankfully, Murdoch is able to expose her ignoble intentions in time. Eaton goes on to marry well and carries on his father's legacy, handing the Eaton empire off to his six children in turn.

**Timothy Eaton** (1834-1907) was a Canadian businessman who founded the Eaton's department store chain in 1869. 509.

Timothy Eaton's presence is felt often in *Murdoch Mysteries*. He puts up the prize for the best invention at the invention convention, promising to sell it in his world-famous department store. In Toronto, his flagship store employs hundreds of men and women, including a group of shopgirls in the ladies wear department. When a murder sends the department into panic, Murdoch unmasks the villainous Eva Pearce, who comes back to haunt him time and again.

**Thomas Edison** (1847-1931), the son of a Canadian from Nova Scotia, was an American businessman and inventor. 703, 808.

Thomas Edison could have been great friends with Murdoch, had his egotistical attitude not spoilt Murdoch's attempts at scientific conversation. Edison continually finds himself on the wrong side of Murdoch's investigations. Though never guilty of murder, his morally questionable practice of patenting the ideas of others tends to put him directly in the line of fire.

*Thomas Edison Jr* (1876-1935) was the eldest son of Thomas Edison and put his name on a great many questionable commercial inventions for profit. 808.

Edison Jr may have lacked the scientific smarts of his father, but he didn't lack business sense. He capitalized on his famous name and made plenty of money hawking the fraudulent inventions of others, to his father's great dismay. However, when implicated in a murder over one such invention, Murdoch manages to negotiate a peace between them – Edison Jr will stop using the famous name on quack products, and Edison senior will pay him a monthly stipend. Unfortunately, Edison Jr goes on with his schemes, just under different names, with varying degrees of success.

*Frederick Fetherstonhaugh* (1863-1945), a patent attorney from Mimico, was a co-founder of the Toronto Automobile Club, had one of the first electrified homes in Toronto and the first electric car in Ontario, created by William Joseph Still in 1893. 805.

*W.C. Fields* (1880-1946) was an American comedian, actor, juggler and writer who began his career in 1898. 809.

Thank goodness for W.C. Fields that he tried to ply his juggling skills in Toronto, whereupon the murder of the monologist gave him the opportunity to try his hand at stand-up comedy. Higgins gives him the boost he needs, finding him rather funny while offstage, though he's unconvinced about the voice Fields tries out – which becomes his trademark as he goes on to huge fame and success.

*Scott Beaudin (Thomas Edison, Jr) and Yannick Bisson shoot a scene at the Medical Emporium and Exhibition set at the Walper Hotel in Kitchener, ON (808).*

Henry Ford (1863-1947) was an American industrialist, and founder of the Ford Motor Company in 1903. 506.

When Murdoch meets him, Ford is in the early stages of developing his combustible motor, and loses handily to James Pendrick's futuristic electric car in a race. But Ford is proven right in the long run – cars that run on gasoline are the wave of the future. Though Ford had more than a little help from the oil conglomerates in making Pendrick's vision disappear and his become reality, had Murdoch not stopped Pendrick from seizing back his patents, Ford's cars may have never gone beyond his prototype, and we would all be driving the Pendrick Bullet instead!

Emma Goldman (1869-1940) was a Russian-born American-Canadian anarchist writer and philosopher. 504, 715.

Emma Goldman's anarchic views on politics made her both a giver of hope and a potential enemy to the state. She always promoted peaceful demonstration and peaceable resistance, but many of her followers took her words in a different context. Implicated in bombings and assassinations, Emma Goldman finds herself a suspect in Toronto, though her innocence always prevails. While in the city, she opens Murdoch's mind to a different perspective, and helps him to realize that her anarchists are not terrorists, but people trying to make a better world for us all.

Margaret Haile (b.-d. unknown) was the first woman to run for public office in the British Empire. 801, 802, 806, 808, 810, 816, 817.

A socialist, Haile believed that socialism and suffrage went hand in hand. When Ogden decides not to run for the Provincial Parliament of Ontario herself, Haile is happy to step in. Running on a platform of suffrage and human equality in the riding of North Toronto, Haile wins seventy-four votes. Considering that all the voters are men, the ladies can't help but be thrilled with their achievement. Who knows if Agnes MacPhail would have fought twenty years later to become Canada's first female Member of Parliament had she not witnessed what Ogden, Grace, Margaret Haile and Lillian Moss did that day at the polls!

Harry Houdini, born Erik Weisz (1874-1926), was a Hungarian-born American illusionist and escape artist performer. 204.

Houdini is at the beginning of his illustrious career when his small show brings him and his brother to Toronto. Of course his beautiful assistant is none other than Ogden's precocious younger sister, Ruby. And of course the bank next door is robbed and a guard killed while Houdini was missing from the stage. But Murdoch proves him innocent, and frees him to become one of the world's greatest magicians.

*Left: Margaret Haile (Nicole Underhay) celebrates on election day with Ogden and Grace (817).*

*Main: Henry Ford (Todd Hofley) prepares for the race (506).*

*Jack the Ripper* was an unidentified serial killer in late nineteenth century London, circa 1888. 202.

Murdoch can't help but believe that visiting Detective Edward Scanlon of Scotland Yard or, in fact, Harlan Orgill, is likely Jack the Ripper himself. Ogden is Orgill's next target, but being the quick-thinker she is, she manages to kill him, and the world is thus rid of one of the most notorious serial killers ever known, though it can never be proven conclusively.

*The Jubilee Singers* (est. 1878) were an all-African-Canadian group of singers, most from the Hamilton area of Ontario, famous worldwide for their renditions of classic plantation songs. 710.

*Sir Wilfred Laurier* (1841-1919) was the seventh Canadian Prime Minister 1896-1911. 407.

Directly in charge of Canadian agent Terrence Meyers, Laurier appears at a time of particular delicacy with their great neighbour to the south. Confronted by a desk sergeant who doesn't even recognize him (played by the twenty-second Prime Minister of Canada, Stephen Harper), Laurier's trip to Station No. 4 is short and to the point. A great honour for Murdoch, but with great honour comes great responsibility…

*Jack London* (1876-1916) was an American writer, journalist, and social and animal activist. 501.

Murdoch's foray into gold panning in the Klondike region of Yukon takes a turn when an innocent woman is arrested for murder. Alone and friendless, Murdoch finds an ally in Jack London, there trying to make his fortune. London saves Murdoch's hide in a bar fight, and Murdoch repays him by supplying the title for the book that will make London a household name, *The Call of the Wild* (1903).

The Jubilee Singers: Chloe Peters (Miranda Edwards), Jeremy Hardy (Dalmar Abuzeid), Ozzy Hughes (Clé Bennett), Buddy Duncan (Ronnie Rowe) and Hattie Carter (Tenika Davis) (710).

Bat Masterson (Steven Ogg) and Murdoch run for cover (803).

_Guglielmo Marconi_ (1874-1937) was an Italian electrical engineer and the inventor of the radio. 708.

Knowing Newfoundland would be the closest point of North American to Europe, Marconi sets out to find a place from which to attempt his wireless signal transmission. If he hadn't then fortuitously bumped into Murdoch and Jacob Doyle, he may not have found the aptly named Signal Hill, and the transmission may not have successfully been made!

_Clara Brett Martin_ (1874-1923) was a Canadian and the first female lawyer in the British Empire. 802, 806, 817.

Martin passed the Ontario bar in 1897 and settled into a quiet practice behind the scenes, having been told her presence in a courtroom would be too disruptive. However, Ogden knows a female lawyer is exactly what her band of suffragettes needs to prove the charges of assault ridiculous. Perhaps Ogden inspires Clara Brett Martin to speak out in favour of suffrage and continue to campaign on behalf of the vote, until the day it is finally granted.

_Clara Brett Martin (Patricia Fagan), the first female lawyer in the British Empire, enters the courtroom (802)._

_William Barclay "Bat" Masterson_ (1853-1921) was an American gunslinger, lawman, hunter, gambler and sports journalist. 803.

Bat Masterson comes to Toronto to cover George "Little Chocolate" Dixon, the Canadian boxing sensation, when he believes he has spotted his lifelong quest – Butch Cassidy and the Sundance Kid. He enlists Murdoch and Brackenreid to help him find the wanted men, and gets them all into a gunslinging shoot-out worthy of any classic western.

_Charles Arthur McCool_ (1853-1926) was the Canadian Member of Parliament for Nipissing 1900-1908, during the railroad expansion and Cobalt silver rush. 811.

_William McKinley_ (1843-1901) was an American soldier and the twenty-fifth President of the United States 1897-1901, who was assassinated while in office. 715.

His assassination had consequences throughout the world. In Toronto, as a result, Terrence Meyers begins a manhunt and the collection of information on private citizens, and Station No. 4 becomes the hub of spy intrigue between nations.

Oliver Mowat (1820-1903) was a Canadian politician, the third Premier of Ontario and the eighth Lieutenant Governor of Ontario, and one of the fathers of Canadian confederation. 607.

Though there are legends of ghosts haunting the Ontario Legislature building at Queen's Park, Sir Oliver Mowat (played by David Onley, twenty-eighth Lieutenant Governor of Ontario) has never seen one himself. But Crabtree believes that was the reason for a death in the building, and he's proven right. In a manner of speaking…

Annie Oakley, born Phoebe Ann Mosey (1860-1926), was an American sharpshooter and Wild West show performer, most notably in Buffalo Bill's Wild West exhibitions. 201.

Annie Oakley catches Brackenreid's eye when Buffalo Bill's travelling show comes to Toronto. A feisty firebrand and a crack shot, she must be considered as a suspect in the murder of one of her fellow showmen. But not before she drinks Brackenreid under the table – the only guest character ever to do so in the eight years of the show!

John Ross Robertson (1841-1918) was a Canadian newspaper publisher, politician and philanthropist who was considered the father of amateur hockey. 512.

Theodore Roosevelt (1858-1919) was an American writer, soldier, naturalist and the twenty-sixth President of the United States. 805.

New York is a bold choice for Murdoch and Ogden to honeymoon. A bustling city with museums, restaurants and nightlife, it is not necessarily what we might expect of our favourite newlyweds. Theodore Roosevelt is certainly grateful they didn't choose to stay on their side of the border, however. Foiling an assassination attempt, Murdoch and Ogden save the American president, and allow children for generations thereafter to enjoy the Teddy Bear, so named after Roosevelt in 1902.

Sam Steele (1848-1919) was an officer of the North West Mounted Police (later the Royal Canadian Mounted Police) and oversaw the Yukon during the Klondike Gold Rush, making it one of the most orderly of its kind. 501.

Annie Taylor (1838-1921) was an American who at age sixty-one was the first person to survive a barrel ride over Niagara Falls. 701.

While in Toronto on a speaking tour, Annie Taylor's barrel is stolen and it's up to Crabtree to find out who took it. The barrel is her livelihood, after all. She went over the falls to help change her fortunes, and now she is forced to travel around and show it off, making barely enough to clothe and feed herself. Thankfully, Crabtree finds her barrel,

*Brackenreid watches Annie Oakley (Sarah Strange) take the perfect shot (201).*

*Speaker of the House (MPP and Speaker of the House Dave Levac), Sir Oliver Mowat (The Honourable David C. Onley, Lieutenant Governor of Ontario) and Crabtree discuss the body (607).*

*Did You Know?*

*In the season 2 premiere, 'Mild Mild West', Yannick really lassoed his target – no stunt double required!*

Main: Archie Milner (Julian Robino) and Marshall Taylor (Dewshane Williams) take their mark (702).
Left: Murdoch ducks for cover as Nikola Tesla (Dmitry Chepovetsky) makes sparks fly in his laboratory (101).

and Annie continues her city tours for many years to come.

Marshall Taylor (1878-1932) was an African-American cycling world champion and world records setter. 702.

The world of competitive sports in Canada wasn't always colour-blind. Marshall "Major" Taylor manages to break those barriers and compete in races across the continent, without using still-legal stimulants like many of his competitors.

Nikola Tesla (1856-1943) was a Serbian-born American inventor, electrical and engineer and futurist. 101, 313.

If there was ever a man who could make Murdoch's heart flutter, it would be Tesla. Innovative and fearless, Tesla is the truest man of the future Murdoch has ever met. Tesla also respects Murdoch, even taking his idea for a long-distance transmitter and turning it into reality. If Murdoch ever wanted to be anyone else, he would want to be Nikola Tesla. He's only sorry he keeps having to question him in his murder investigations.

Thomas "Tom" Thomson (1877-1917) was a Canadian artist noted for his natural scenes inspired by Algonquin Park, Ontario. 811.

Thomson always wanted to be an artist, but it wasn't until he saw Brackenreid's vivid "essence of the north woods" that he became inspired. Without Brackenreid – and his shortage of green paint – Thomson may never have discovered the trademark style that would influence generations of Canadian artists to come.

H.G. Wells (1866-1946) was an English writer probably best-known for his works of science fiction. 308.

Enjoying the attentions of the younger Ogden sister, Wells is blindsided by the beauty and grace of Julia Ogden, leaving Murdoch to suffer his jealousy in silence. However, implicated in a murder over the eugenicist principles Wells believes in, he leaves a lasting impression on Toronto. He also ignites a slow burn in Murdoch to win back his lady love.

Orville (1871-1948) and Wilfred (1867-1912) Wright were American inventors and aviation pioneers. 601.

Though they had been conducting experiments in flight since 1896, the Wright brothers' airplane doesn't take flight until 1903, meaning Pendrick's Arrow beats them into the air by two years. However, with Pendrick's vision for a better future dashed, he subsequently abandons his dreams of flight, clearing the way for the Wright brothers to secure their place in aviation history.

# A Love
# FOR THE AGES

Dr Julia Ogden *"Life without you, William, it is worse than death."*

Detective William Murdoch *"Listen to me. Together we're stronger than anyone."*

*Murdoch and Ogden study the remains of a human bone found after excavating a farmhouse's basement (305).*

*Opposite: Murdoch interrupts Ogden's breathing exercise class (106).*

# F *A Love* OR THE AGES

There are many great love stories throughout history, and even more in literature, film and television. The saga of William Murdoch and Julia Ogden may just rank up there with the longest, most frustrating, most beautiful, most tormented and most anticipated of all.

Destined for one another from the very first scene of the very first episode, viewers and the show's writers alike have been clamouring ever since for the moment they would finally come together and be happy. That moment arrives in season 8, after a long and tumultuous journey. After all, the greatest lovers are always doomed to suffer before they can achieve true happiness, and Ogden and Murdoch are no exception.

## 1895 ✿✿✿✿✿✿✿✿✿✿✿✿✿✿✿✿✿✿✿✿✿✿✿✿✿✿✿✿✿✿✿✿✿✿✿✿✿✿✿✿✿✿✿✿✿✿✿✿✿✿✿✿✿✿✿✿✿✿✿✿✿✿✿✿✿

Murdoch and Ogden have a lovely working relationship forged over two years since Ogden began working in the City Morgue. Murdoch, now recovered from the death of his fiancee Liza Milner, begins to consider his feelings for Ogden in a new light. She is beyond him socially, but with her, social convention seems to be irrelevant. They continually find out new and interesting things about one another, and their mutual attraction only grows. However, Murdoch, ever the gentleman – and perhaps a little afraid of the strength of his own feelings – is content to keep their contact professional. Ogden, equally committed to her work and likely unwilling to compromise her hard-fought position, allows their relationship to stay within the status quo. But neither can ignore the passion that begins to grow between them.

*Murdoch and Ogden are two big brains rubbing up against each other in a friendly manner.* Cal Coons, *Executive Producer*

*Ogden examines Alice's (Tamsen McDonough) body, while Murdoch checks out the faulty switch (101).*

## 1896 ✿✿✿✿✿✿✿✿✿✿✿✿✿✿✿✿✿✿✿✿✿✿✿✿✿✿✿✿✿✿✿✿✿✿✿✿✿✿✿✿✿✿✿✿✿✿✿✿✿✿✿✿✿✿✿✿✿✿✿✿✿✿✿✿✿

Murdoch and Ogden enjoy a sweet, gentlemanly courtship. They attend lectures, scientific exhibits, and discuss technology and medicine and crime. They fit together perfectly, despite their social differences, and they are happy. Their lives are full of promise.

*After taking dance lessons, Murdoch and Odgen show off their moves on the dance floor (203).*

Did You Know?

The theme music for Murdoch and Ogden's romance was originally written for episode 101 'Power', as the background music to Crabtree and Edna.

*After a dead body is found in the i*

Main: Murdoch and Anna Fulford (Lisa Faulkner) take a ride through the streets in Bristol (301).

Right: Murdoch climbs up a hot air balloon to win over Ogden (213).

Then Murdoch takes on a case involving the death of a woman who wished to abort her illegitimate child. The evidence leads to an old friend of Dr Ogden, Dr Tash. Seeing the two doctors together, Tash becomes the subject of Murdoch's intense jealousy, but when he confronts Ogden she can only ask him to leave it be. Murdoch is not one for secrets, though, and forces Ogden's hand. She admits to him that when she was in university, a dalliance with a man led to a pregnancy, which she terminated. She almost died at the hand of a butcher, and Tash saved her life. Murdoch's shock at this admission is palpable. He loves this woman more than he imagined possible, but Ogden has not only broken the law, she chose to do something which to him has always been unthinkable. Perhaps worst of all, she does not regret her actions. Their mutual inability to share their feelings only exacerbates the issue, and they part, their fledgling relationship now in tatters.

In the course of another investigation, Murdoch meets a young widow, Enid Jones, and her son Alwyn. He sees in them the family he has always wanted, without complication or compromise. He begins to court Enid, but though their relationship is sweet, it is without passion. So much so that Murdoch can't help but fantasize about Ogden, and she about him, during the course of their investigations. Enid seems more of a comfort to Murdoch, a way to return his confused heart to a normal, solid, steady beat. After several weeks of pleasant calm, Murdoch realizes his heart still belongs, and always will, to Ogden. Enid can't help but notice their attraction and asks Murdoch to choose. Murdoch knows he has no real choice. Ogden is his true love. He and Enid must part.

Murdoch tries to tell Ogden that he would like to start again, but Ogden is otherwise engaged with a Mr Reginald Poundsett. Again Murdoch's jealousy rears up and he asks Crabtree to find out everything he can about Ogden's new supposed suitor. What Crabtree discovers gives Murdoch new hope. Ogden has been taking ballooning lessons, and he rushes to find her, jumping into the basket, happy to go wherever the winds may take them, as long as they are together.

**1897** ✤✤✤✤✤✤✤✤✤✤✤✤✤✤✤✤✤✤✤✤✤✤✤✤✤✤✤✤✤✤✤✤✤✤✤✤✤✤✤✤✤✤✤✤✤✤✤✤✤✤✤✤✤✤✤✤✤✤✤✤✤✤✤

Murdoch, hot on the heels of a murderer, is attacked and wakes without any memory of who he is or where he was going. A steamer ticket in his pocket takes him to Bristol, where he is fortuitously rescued by a plucky barmaid, the lovely and irrepressible Anna Fulford. An attraction between the two is obvious from the start, and this baggage-free version of William has none of his Catholic upbringing nor any of his customary conservative reticence. We see William free from his bonds, free of his torment with Ogden, and free to be comfortable as any man would be confronted by a beautiful woman tending to his wounds.

Soon Murdoch's memories begin to return, and with them his Victorian sensibilities. He manages, albeit barely, to stay the consummate gentleman, despite Anna's very real temptation, finds the murderer and returns, perhaps with some small regret, to his life in Toronto.

Any regret quickly disappears when he is greeted by a tearful and relieved Ogden. Their heartfelt embrace sets the tone for their relationship in the months to come. Together, the issue of her abortion now in the past, Murdoch and Ogden continue on their courtship.

But the calm doesn't last. When a corpse on her table suddenly jumps to life and threatens her, Ogden begins to reconsider her career path. The morgue may be fascinating, but her years of struggle to become a doctor have yet to help the living. When she is offered a position at a new children's hospital in Buffalo, she finds herself having a hard time finding a reason to turn it down. Murdoch is surprised – he had thought things were going well between them. Ogden confesses the burden she has been carrying. The abortion rendered her sterile, and it's been obvious to her for some time that Murdoch desperately wants children. She has been too terrified of losing him to tell him the truth. Murdoch, in typical fashion, says nothing.

Busy on a case of global importance, Murdoch has yet to tell Ogden that he would rather spend his life with her than have a biological child, leaving Ogden feeling she has no reason to stay. To her the relationship with Murdoch has no chance of moving forward, and Buffalo offers a fresh start. She makes a decision to accept the position, and Murdoch, delayed by the purchase of an engagement ring, arrives too late to stop her.

*Kevin Bundy (Dr Martin Falwell) shoots a scene with Hélène Joy and Yannick Bisson (403).*

*Ogden and Murdoch encounter Laetecia Abbot (Tammy Isbell, standing) and Dr Darcy Garland (Jonathan Watton) with a patient(Mikaela Bisson) (403).*

*Main: Dr Llewllyn Francis (Paul Rhys) and Murdoch work together reluctantly (402).*

*Right: Ogden and Murdoch share an intimate moment (302).*

Murdoch and Ogden examine Randolph Littlefair's murder scene the night after the Alice in Wonderland costume party (413).

Murdoch interprets Ogden's departure as a message to stay away, and attempts instead to throw himself into his work. The new coroner, Dr Llewellyn Francis, is hardly Ogden, and Murdoch takes his frustrations out on the unpleasant yet capable man.

In reality, Ogden can't stay away from Murdoch any more than he can her, and she asks him to come to Buffalo and help her solve a mystery. Their reunion is effortless, and they slip back into their investigative partnership with ease. Murdoch attempts to propose yet again, but Ogden stops him. She is already engaged to be married, to Dr Darcy Garland.

Murdoch is completely flummoxed, but swallows his hurt and confusion and congratulates her. Ogden knows Murdoch wants children, something she has been told she can never give him. She does not know he is willing to adopt. She doesn't believe she can make him happy, and that breaks her heart. So she forces herself to move on, and finds a sympathetic man in Darcy, who accepts her past and her present. In this way she hopes to find some happiness, if of a lesser kind, and hopes to give Murdoch the freedom to find his. Murdoch cannot understand her decision, but he accepts it quietly and without fuss, much to everyone's frustration, both on screen and at home.

With Ogden's return to the morgue after only a brief departure, the year progresses awkwardly. Murdoch and Ogden can work together, but neither can suppress their feelings completely. As the day of Ogden's wedding approaches, her sister Ruby persuades her to tell Murdoch of her feelings. But Murdoch is in jail, and events conspire against them. He doesn't receive her note asking him to demonstrate his true feelings until it is almost too late. Finding himself faced with a moral dilemma of staggering proportions, he chooses to atone for a past wrong against a murderess for whom he feels responsible, rather than stop Ogden's wedding. Ogden, hearing nothing back from Murdoch, takes a deep breath and decides to move forward with her life, turning her back on Murdoch, and saying "I do" to Darcy Garland.

Ogden, now married, resumes her duties in the morgue. With Murdoch absent she doesn't initially know if they can go on working together. However, when he returns it's immediately apparent that what she and Murdoch have is enduring, and impossible to ignore. Consequently, she decides to leave the morgue and its daily reminder of a life she believes she can't have, instead setting up a private practice while Darcy takes a prominent position at the Victoria Hospital for Sick Children. She hands over the morge to Emily Grace, and does her best to stay out of the business of the police.

It's not long before Ogden's unconventional approach to her women's clinic, specifically teaching illegal contraception, puts her behind the bars of Station No. 4. Darcy can't persuade her to stop her flagrant contravention of the law, and Murdoch knows better than to try. For the first time Ogden is aware of Darcy's reticence to support her as she tries to change the world, a reticence that will soon grow into resolve, and open a chasm between them that will never be bridged.

Murdoch, meanwhile, has done his best to accept Ogden's decision. His foray to the Yukon at the beginning of the year helped reaffirm what was important in his life, and he meets more than one woman who appears interested. The arrival of Anna Fulford in Toronto comes at a welcome time for Murdoch, and coincides with Ogden's arrest. Murdoch entertains the idea of a future with Anna for the first time, though circumstances with the Black Hand ultimately make it impossible. For her part, Ogden finally sees that Murdoch has moved on, and further resigns herself to the life she has chosen.

Then a terrifying series of threatening dolls sent by the villain James Gillies reveals a plot to persecute Murdoch, culminating in the kidnap and live burial of Ogden as his ultimate torment. Murdoch rescues Ogden and she falls into his arms, sobbing. Their true feelings laid bare for a moment, and the inevitability of their love made painfully apparent to everyone, in this one poignant moment, everything has changed yet again. Ogden knows she cannot stay with Darcy, and Darcy is beginning to see the truth as well. He tells her to start the new century with the man she wants.

In one of the most-watched scenes in the entire series, Ogden appears at the Policeman's New Year's Ball in a stunning gown, approaching Murdoch nervously. She tells him she and Darcy have parted, almost too terrified to look at him for his response. Murdoch, despite the scandal, and without even a thought to propriety, catches her in an impassioned embrace, oblivious to the crowd and the fireworks around them. Their future will be rocky, but they will be together. Of this there can no longer be even the shadow of a doubt.

## 1900

Their close friends and colleagues know Murdoch and Ogden are together, even if the couple attempt to keep it relatively private while she extricates herself from her marriage. Ogden cannot bring herself to annul the marriage, as she would be forced to lie about Darcy's conduct on the record, which could affect his career and public standing. So a divorce it must be, where she will take all of the blame and the social consequence. She

*Murdoch and Dr Ogden kiss at the Policeman's Ball (513).*

707).

*Ogden awaits her hanging (613).*

*Brackenreid and Crabtree save Murdoch (613).*

*Hélène Joy shooting a tense moment for Ogden (613).*

is, after all, the one who wants to end their marriage. Darcy is just collateral damage in the saga of Murdoch and Ogden. But a divorce is not an easy feat in Victorian Toronto. There are several steps involved, including great expense and public announcements in the newspapers exposing all the sordid details. As the first step is to prove infidelity, Ogden contrives to falsify an affair with a stranger, but Murdoch won't allow it. If Ogden's name is to be dragged through the mud, then it will be dragged along with his. They are together, in this and in everything.

Before Ogden can even complete the first step and place her fabricated evidence in the newspaper, however, Darcy changes his mind. He will not grant Ogden a divorce after all. He no longer wishes to weather the storm of scandal it will cause, even if he is seen to be an innocent victim in the whole affair. His star is on the rise in Toronto and he refuses to allow her to ruin his career as well as his home.

Ogden and Murdoch are at a loss. Ogden is ready to give up on society all together and live in sin with Murdoch, hang their careers! Murdoch, of course, loves her too much to allow it. They will be together properly, somehow, and Ogden loves him all the more for staying true to himself, and to her.

*Love comes hard for these protagonists because they're oddballs.*

Cal Coons, *Executive Producer*

They are at a standstill, though firmly committed to one another. Until the day that Darcy Garland is murdered in his home – by a woman who looks exactly like Julia Ogden. Murdoch fights for her, though the evidence condemns her to the noose. Only then does James Gillies reveal himself as the crime's mastermind. It was an experiment on an emotion he himself is incapable of feeling, love.

With the clock ticking down to both Murdoch's death at the hand of Gillies and Ogden's hanging, Murdoch agrees to make the ultimate sacrifice, his life for that of the one he loves. Thankfully Brackenreid and Crabtree have discovered Gillies' scheme and save Murdoch, who then races to save Ogden. Love triumphs over evil yet again.

Though they are now free to be together, the shadow of Darcy's senseless death hangs over them. Ogden knows they aren't responsible for the actions of a sociopathic murderer, but had it not been for their choices – for her choices – Darcy would likely still be alive. Gillies may not have succeeded in exacting his revenge the way he hoped, but he has cast a pall over their immediate future. Both Ogden and Murdoch need a moment to breathe.

## 1901

Ogden and Murdoch are happy to find one another on the maiden voyage of a new passenger vessel on Lake Ontario. Not separated, but not actively courting, the trip feels like a fresh start. Free of the shackles of Ogden's marriage, and both having come to terms with the circumstances of Darcy's death, they find themselves ready to begin again, as though their love is reborn, without all of the baggage of the past years.

### I enjoy how William isn't jaded at all, even to a fault.

Yannick Bisson, *Detective William Murdoch*

Murdoch and Ogden subsequently spend many lovely days together, experiencing one another as though for the first time. Even the appearance of Leslie Garland, Darcy's younger brother, doesn't seem to affect them. The death of James Gillies while escaping from the train transporting him to his execution, though grim, gives Murdoch and Ogden closure on that terrible chapter of their relationship.

Then Ogden receives a threatening note from Gillies, whom she thought was dead, warning her to stay away from Murdoch. Old terrors are inflamed. Determined to find the truth without putting Murdoch's life in jeopardy again, Ogden places herself in harm's way, only to find Gillies one step ahead. Ogden is now so afraid she doesn't dare tell Murdoch, and is forced to say no to his long-awaited proposal of marriage.

She finally tells Murdoch the truth, and together they uncover Leslie Garland masquerading as Gillies, a cruel joke as a way of avenging his brother's death. But instead of anger, Ogden feels only relief. Gillies is dead, Leslie is exposed, and she and Murdoch feel free, truly free. After everything they have been through, there is nothing in their future that can tear them apart ever again.

Murdoch sits on his proposal of marriage, waiting for the right moment. It arrives after the death of Ogden's father, by the picturesque lake of her family cottage. She tells him to ask her again. He does. She says yes. Ogden and Murdoch are engaged to be married. After seven long years of ups and down, tears and laughter, they can finally be together as man and wife.

*Main: The cargo hold set, built in a swimming pool (701).*

*Above: Ogden is desperate to find Murdoch (701).*

*Left: Yannick Bisson prepares for his underwater shoot with Hélène Joy (701).*

*Did You Know?*

The writers could never come to a consensus as to whether Murdoch had been intimate with a woman before marriage. Only Murdoch himself knows for sure. The debate in the writers' room rages to this day!

*Ogden and Murdoch decide not to wait a minute longer to get married (718).*

## 1902

Murdoch and Ogden are content in their engagement. Neither is very preoccupied about the ceremony or even the date. Both are busy with work and are happy and secure with each other. With Brackenreid convalescing after his near-fatal beating, more serious matters are on their minds. Ogden is concerned with Brackenreid's mental health, and Murdoch has yet to catch the person who attacked him. It doesn't seem quite the right time to celebrate.

Soon enough, though, the other issues are resolved. So, with Brackenreid back on the force, and the criminal behind bars, Murdoch and Ogden begin the wedding planning. That is, Mrs Brackenreid begins the wedding planning and Ogden is happy to let her do so, or has no other choice.

The wedding isn't without its hiccups, but Brackenreid refuses to allow the happy couple to leave the premises until they are officially married, smart man that he is, and thus it happens. Dr Ogden becomes Mrs Murdoch – but only when necessary for convenience's sake – and they are free to live on, married and happy.

We see them in their domestic setting, as comfortable with one another as though they had been married for years. A long time coming, their quiet happiness is well deserved.

Though their story is still far from over…

*Main: Murdoch and Ogden at the altar (804).*

*Right: Murdoch and Ogden share a smile over breakfast in their hotel suite (808).*

# Celebrating a Milestone
## THE 100ᵀᴴ EPISODE

**Dr Julia Ogden** *"I think this has been the perfect wedding day."*

**Detective William Murdoch** *"With one exception. I have yet to kiss the bride."*

*Previous spread: Murdoch and Ogden at the altar.*

*Main and left: On location in Cambridge.*

*Below: Murdoch and Ogden chase down the suspects in their wedding carriage.*

# From Idea to Script
## THE 100ᵀᴴ EPISODE

Every year, the writing staff meets several months before the series goes into production. They generate all the stories in the writers' room, bringing in individual ideas, and together coming up with more ideas. They then spend several weeks discussing, researching, "breaking" and writing those ideas into what will eventually become the season ahead. By the time the cameras are ready to roll, the storylines of the season are already in place, and several of them are already written. Of course there is often change, and stories are moved around or replaced with different ones, but for the most part the writers are well prepared for production to begin.

*Crabtree expresses relief as Higgins (Lachlan Murdoch) presents the wedding ring.*

When the writing room first convened to talk about season 8, they knew they had two very important events to consider: the one hundredth episode of the series, and Murdoch and Ogden's much-anticipated wedding.

For the one hundredth episode – a rare milestone in a Canadian series – the writing team knew they had to do something special. Several ideas were kicked around, but the writers quickly realized if Murdoch and Ogden were going to get married, then there would be no more fitting occasion.

Peter Mitchell, Paul Aitken, Carol Hay, Michelle Ricci, Jordan Christianson and Simon McNabb began their brainstorming. They had Murdoch and Ogden's wedding to fill part of the episode, but *Murdoch Mysteries* is just that, a mystery show, so there needed to be an investigation with some twists and turns. Our heroes' wedding would also need some drama, some intrigue, and some potential to fail.

The writers deliberately chose to stay away from anything too melodramatic. They decided against having an arch-enemy appear to thwart Murdoch and Ogden's happiness yet again. The mystery must be unrelated to the two lovers, but would ideally have some emotional resonance. So, just as Murdoch and Ogden are preparing for the happiest day of their lives, they would be confronted by a case that reflects that happiness gone wrong.

*Ogden enters the church with Brackenrede.*

*Ogden and Murdoch interrupt their own wedding.*

The trick would be to balance the two storylines satisfactorily. The audience should enjoy the wedding preparations and the event itself, but still be intrigued by the mystery and ultimately satisfied with the solution of the case and the resolution of Murdoch and Ogden's long courtship.

The writers felt there would be nothing more true to the characters than to have the case interfere in the ceremony. Of course Murdoch's brain would find the clue in the middle of his own wedding, and of course Ogden would be caught up in the thrill of solving the mystery with him. For one excruciating moment, the viewer is confronted with the reality that Murdoch and Ogden are both about to walk out on their own wedding to stop a murderer, after over seven years of the audience's angst-ridden waiting – and we fully believe that the happy couple will really leave. But, true to form, Brackenreid is the audience's voice, having similarly suffered through Murdoch and Ogden's long saga. Murderer or no, he refuses to allow the couple to leave the church until they say their vows. For the writers, this was the perfect *Murdoch Mysteries* wedding. Murdoch and Ogden, whose romance bloomed through solving cases and was strengthened by their joint curiosity and desire to find the truth, would be ready to abandon their own wedding without a second thought and Brackenreid would stop them, refusing to suffer any more delays for his own sanity, if not the happy couple's. It fit with everyone's characters, gave the episode the drama it would need to be successful, managed to avoid melodrama and added a pinch of humour through the circumstance. The writers were satisfied and began their usual process of turning those scattered bones into a fully fleshed-out script.

*Brackenreid and Margaret (Arwen Humphreys) are not impressed when the wedding is interrupted.*

# THE WEDDING DRESS

Ogden's wedding dress in season 8 was a challenge because it had to look special and also be enough of a departure from her previous dress, worn for her marriage to Dr Darcy Garland in season 4.

The design process began with researching weddings of the period and fashion books of the period specific to weddings. I then took different elements from different dresses and compiled them to see which ones would work best for Dr Ogden's character and suit the actress, Hélène Joy, best as well.

Once this was achieved, I did a series of drawings for about twelve different dresses and after much deliberation and consultation with the producers and director we agreed on the one chosen. It best reflected her in its strength, simplicity and yet had enough romance about it to make it special. I didn't want it to be too frothy; beautiful but understated.

We began by drafting the patterns and making a cotton mock-up for a first fitting to get a sense of the proportions and fit. While this was happening fabric was sourced, as well as lace trim and beading. The added challenge was that we would need to build a second dress for a riding double (a stunt actor who could double for Ogden while riding the horse) and the train had to be removable for Hélène's comfort in between takes and to be able to jump onto a horse.

Each dress used twenty metres of silk, twenty-five metres of lace trim for the skirt and five metres of veiling. We also built a special petticoat to make the skirt stand more fully and we made a special bum- and hip-pad to give the correct silhouette to the skirt. It was less revealing than Ogden's first dress, where skin was shown through the organza. It's a second marriage and modesty was more important. There was also some discussion as to whether the dress should be white, but in the end cream was the appropriate choice.

*– Alex Reda, Costume Designer*

*Top: Alex Reda's costume design (left) and the final dress (right).*

*Above: Ogden walks down the aisle.*

*Left: A close-up of the wedding dress train.*

*Far left: Executive Producer/Shaftesbury CEO Christina Jennings greets costume designer Alex Reda, carrying Dr Ogden's wedding dress to Metropolitan United Church.*

Ogden

Wedding Dress

Paul Aitken was chosen to write that script. As the only writer to have worked on the entire series from the first episode, it was most fitting he be the one to finally bring Murdoch and Ogden together in the episode titled 'Holy Matrimony, Murdoch!'. The writers then began to "break" or "beat out" the story. This is when the writers all work together to lay out the story from beginning to end, with all the specifics – or "beats" – of what should happen in each scene, and in which order the scenes should play. They discuss the clues and the evidence, making sure that all of the investigation follows a logical and interesting path, leading to the conclusion. They also find places for the investigation to veer off, or lay in red herrings or dead ends. This becomes the skeleton that the entire episode will be built around. It is both the most crucial and the most difficult part of the process and can take anywhere from two days to a week to complete.

Once the "beat sheet" was finished, Paul took it and wrote the outline, for which the writers on *Murdoch Mysteries* generally have a week. He used the beat sheet as his guide, and filled in whatever holes remained, turning a few pages of bullet points into about fifteen pages of prose, with each scene defined and written in paragraph form. This was then read by the writers and revised before being sent to the network for approval.

Once approved, Paul then took the outline and wrote it out as the script, with those fifteen pages of prose becoming a fifty-nine-page first draft. That was then given to the writers' room, who in turn gave Paul another set of notes. He then revised the first draft, which was then sent to the network for their notes. This became the "production draft", and the script was ready for the production team to start their work to bring it to the screen.

*I've seen* Murdoch Mysteries *grow from a period when the only buzz around it was the flies on the craft table to a Twitter-verse that just can't keep its hands to itself. I've even been asked to sign autograph books and pose for pictures, though I am just the boom operator.*

David Horton, *Boom Operator*

Hundreds of people work to bring each episode of *Murdoch Mysteries* into being, and millions of fans enjoy watching the fruits of their labour. A magic alchemy of writing, casting, setting, costuming, directing, editing, scoring and enhancing has made this unique gem of a show into a worldwide phenomenon. Loved by cast, crew and fans alike, we are all grateful for its 114 episodes to rewatch and look forward to the horrors and delights yet to grace our screens in the years to come.

*Murdoch and Dr Ogden arrive at their wedding reception.*

*Ogden and Murdoch share their first kiss as husband and wife.*